REBUS'S FAVOURITE
THE DEUCHARS GUIDE TO EDINBURGH PUBS

BY TOM BRUCE–GARDYNE
& JOHN SKINNER
WITH A FOREWORD BY
IAN RANKIN
LINE DRAWINGS BY TOM BRUCE–GARDYNE

This Deuchars Guide is dedicated to the memory of my dear friend and
fellow writer John Skinner who sadly died before the book was finished.
Tom Bruce-Gardyne

1

CONTENTS

An Orion paperback. First published in Great Britain
in 2007 by Orion Books Ltd,
Orion House, 5 Upper St Martin's Lane
London WC2H 9EA

An Hachette Livre UK company

1 3 5 7 9 10 8 6 4 2

ISBN 978-0-7528-9521-5.
Designed by Tourist
Printed and bound in Great Britain by CPD

The Orion Publishing Group's policy is to use papers
that are natural, renewable and recyclable products
and made from wood grown in sustainable forests.
The logging and manufacturing processes are expected
to conform to the environmental regulations of the
country of origin.

www.caledonian-brewery.co.uk
www.orionbooks.co.uk
www.ianrankin.net

FOREWORD
IAN RANKIN

God, I love pubs. Not all pubs are created equal, of course, and I do have my preferences. What I really like though is the idea of 'the pub' as a place of good conversation, democratic spirit, a few laughs, relaxation, and community. When I enter a new pub for the first time, I'll be on the lookout for certain clues. Postcards pinned up behind the bar mean the clients like the place enough to remember it when they head off on holiday. Other notices may include a golf trip for regulars, or a pool league, or even the dreaded karaoke night – all are evidence that the pub in question has become more than just a place to quench a thirst.

A good boozer should be like a club with an open-door policy. The first time you order a drink, you're a stranger; next time you go back, the bar staff remember what you asked for last time; after a further visit, you're on first-name terms and have come a respectable third in the dominoes tourney.

My ideal pub would be fairly quiet during the day, allowing me to read the paper in peace, but lively at lunch-time and after work. I'm one of that rare breed who can sit in a pub all day and call it 'work' – maybe because I'm planning my next book in my head, or looking for ideas, characters, anecdotes and stories. Centuries back, this was the way it worked in Edinburgh. If you wanted to talk to a lawyer, you would seek them in the back rooms of their favoured howffs. A corner table would be their desk, paperwork set before them. The city's advocates would rub shoulders with harlots, poets and pickpockets. Songs might be sung and fiddles scratched. All were welcome, as long as they had about their person the price of that next drink.

The town where I grew up boasted two Gothenburgs. My dad drank at one of these 'Goths', though my friends and I preferred the Auld Hoose. This latter boasted tabletop video games such as Space Invaders, plus a dartboard and pool table – mod cons my father's generation could do without. And now that I am my father's generation, I find that I, too, can do without bells and whistles. I don't mind the rippling sound of daytime television (horse-racing; *Countdown;* the History Channel), but try to avoid loud music and too many 'puggies'. To me, a visit to the pub is a social occasion. Jokes and news will be shared, politics discussed. Someone will be letting off steam about their job, while their neighbour rants about the state of the roads and pavements. The bar staff will listen patiently, like therapists.

I arrived in Edinburgh aged eighteen to study at university. My first drinks would have been in the Student Union bars and on Rose Street pub-crawls. But I soon learned which pubs suited me. In my second year, I stayed in a flat at Tollcross, and drank in Bennets. One memorable night, I bought a drink for the poet Norman MacCaig, and was rewarded with an hour of insight and humour. A few years later, as a postgraduate, I was introduced to the Oxford Bar by a flatmate who worked there part-time. Tucked away down a narrow lane in the city centre, it seemed to represent the 'hidden Edinburgh' that I was trying to write about. In time, I decided that my main character, Detective Inspector John Rebus, would make it his local, and would favour the same tipple as his creator, namely Deuchar's IPA.

In fact, just writing these words has given me a 'drouth'. Time to do some exploring, armed with the very book you're holding.

CHEERS!

4

EDINBURGH, DEUCHARS IPA, RANKIN AND REBUS

Whether you live in Edinburgh or are simply visiting, step outside, close your eyes and take a deep sniff. When the wind is blowing in the right direction, the sweet and sour aroma of freshly brewed beer is unmistakable especially when the air is cold and damp. This is the smell of Edinburgh and has been almost from the start. At one point the city was bathed in the beery fumes of over forty commercial breweries. Today there is just one, and if you follow your nose you will find it out west on Slateford Road. The Caledonian Brewery, or the Caley as it is popularly known, has survived against all odds. Much bigger breweries pumping out much bigger brands have been bulldozed into history – the most recent being the giant Fountain Brewery, which closed in 2004.

The Caley is home to Deuchars – which is to Edinburgh what Guinness has long been to Dublin. Because the Caledonian Brewery has no tied houses of its own, none of the city's 500-plus pubs are obliged to take Deuchars IPA or its stable-mate, Caledonian 80/-. The fact that so many do is a tribute to the quality of these prize-winning beers. Plus of course it is only natural for publicans to want to serve the local brew.

For many readers not native to Edinburgh, their first introduction to Deuchars IPA is through Ian Rankin's bestselling Inspector Rebus novels. The workaholic, cynical Detective Inspector John Rebus can generally be found propping up Edinburgh's Oxford Bar with a pint of his favourite beer – Deuchars IPA – in his hand to slake his thirst after a hard day's crime fighting. Ian has long been a fan of Deuchars, so it was only natural that his world-weary fictional inspector would drink it: 'Like Inspector Rebus, I've been drinking Deuchars IPA for more years than I can remember. I loved it from the first time I tasted it, and it seemed the right beer for Rebus – though it helped, of course, that it happened to be stocked on draught at the

Oxford Bar, which is Rebus's local watering-hole as well as my own!' The care that goes into making Deuchars would be wasted in Edinburgh if there were not such a glorious rabble of quirky and eccentric pubs in which to sink a few pints. As with any drink it is where and with whom you are doing the drinking that matters most of all. Even the finest wine or single malt whisky can taste flat if drunk alone in somewhere that is sterile and uninspiring. On this score Deuchars has little to worry about in its home town. Despite many changes over the years, pub culture is alive and kicking in Edinburgh.

What follows is not a pub guide in the established sense with places marked out of ten for their range of real ales or whether they serve food through the day. There has been no attempt to determine the level of 'craic' as the Irish say – as if you could rate such a thing. It is certainly not an exhaustive list either; there was sadly not space to include all the city's good bars. We set out to cover the featured pubs in some detail, peeling away the layers of history and piecing together any cultural references we could find. We wanted to set them in context and try and distil a little of what makes them special and unique. And we wanted to highlight the pubs where not only could you get hold of a pint of 'Rebus's Favourite', but you'd be drinking in a pub or bar that the Inspector himself would choose – he's quite picky about the howffs he chooses to drink in.

As in any city there are some unmemorable or unengaging pubs or vast drinking sheds that heave and sway on a Friday night and could be anywhere. Yet in amongst it all are some real gems. When it comes to really good pubs, Edinburgh is truly blessed, and this little guide will hopefully point you in the right direction.

Go forth and drink!

EDINBURGH – 400 YEARS OF BREWING TRADITION

The history of brewing in Edinburgh dates back to the 12th century when the monks of Holyrood sunk a well at the base of Arthur's Seat, the city's ancient, volcanic peak, and began using the water to make beer.

Unwittingly they had tapped into a large underground lake that was later christened the 'Charmed Circle of Brewing Wells' by the city's brewers. The water was relatively hard, crystal clear and rich in traces of gypsum. Put simply it was perfect for making beer – especially the lighter, well-hopped pale ales that Edinburgh became famous for.

Beer-making evolved slowly out of the monasteries and into the home. By 1596 there were enough people making beer on a commercial scale for the city to form its own Society of Brewers. One early member was John Blair who took over from the monks at Holyrood when they finally stopped brewing in 1600. He was soon supplying the royal residence next door and a wider audience beyond.

A century or more later, brewing was still a cottage industry. For the most part it was a business in the sense that beer made on the premises was sold on the premises as people's houses became 'howffs'. Traditionally it was the women who did the brewing – women like Maggy Johnston who ran a celebrated tavern on the south side of Edinburgh in Bruntsfield. Maggy's death in 1713 moved the poet Allan Ramsay to pen an elegy to her. The opening lines are as follows:

Auld Reeky mourn in sable hue!
Let fouth of tears dreep like Mary-dew!
To braw tippony bid adieu,
Which we with greed
Bended as fast as she could brew:-
But ah! She's dead.

Ae summer nights I was sae fou,*
Amang the riggs I Gaed to spew...
*drunk

All cities specialised in particular trades and centuries of experience gave them an edge over rivals who sought to compete. While Dundee developed into the city of jute, jam and journalism, Edinburgh became the city of beer and bibles – the latter a reference to its long-established printing industry. Brewing began here as a consequence of having easy access to the raw ingredients and plentiful supplies of good water. The craft was perfected by all the subsequent generations of brewers, and by the time the Caledonian Brewery was established in 1869, the art of making good beer was too deeply bred in the bone ever to disappear.

Originally there had been two main styles of Scottish ale. First there was 'dark and heavy' which weighed in at around 11% alcohol by volume and was colloquially known as 'nappy'. It features in Robert Burns' 'Tam o' Shanter' with the lines 'while we sit bousing at the nappy an' getting fou an' unco happy.' Then there was 'Small Ale' which was made by brewing up the old grains from the Scotch Ale a second time, which made it much lighter and about half the strength. It was drunk with meals as a refreshing and safe alternative to town water. The increasing use of English grain and especially English hops was pioneered by the Edinburgh brewers and improved the end result no end.

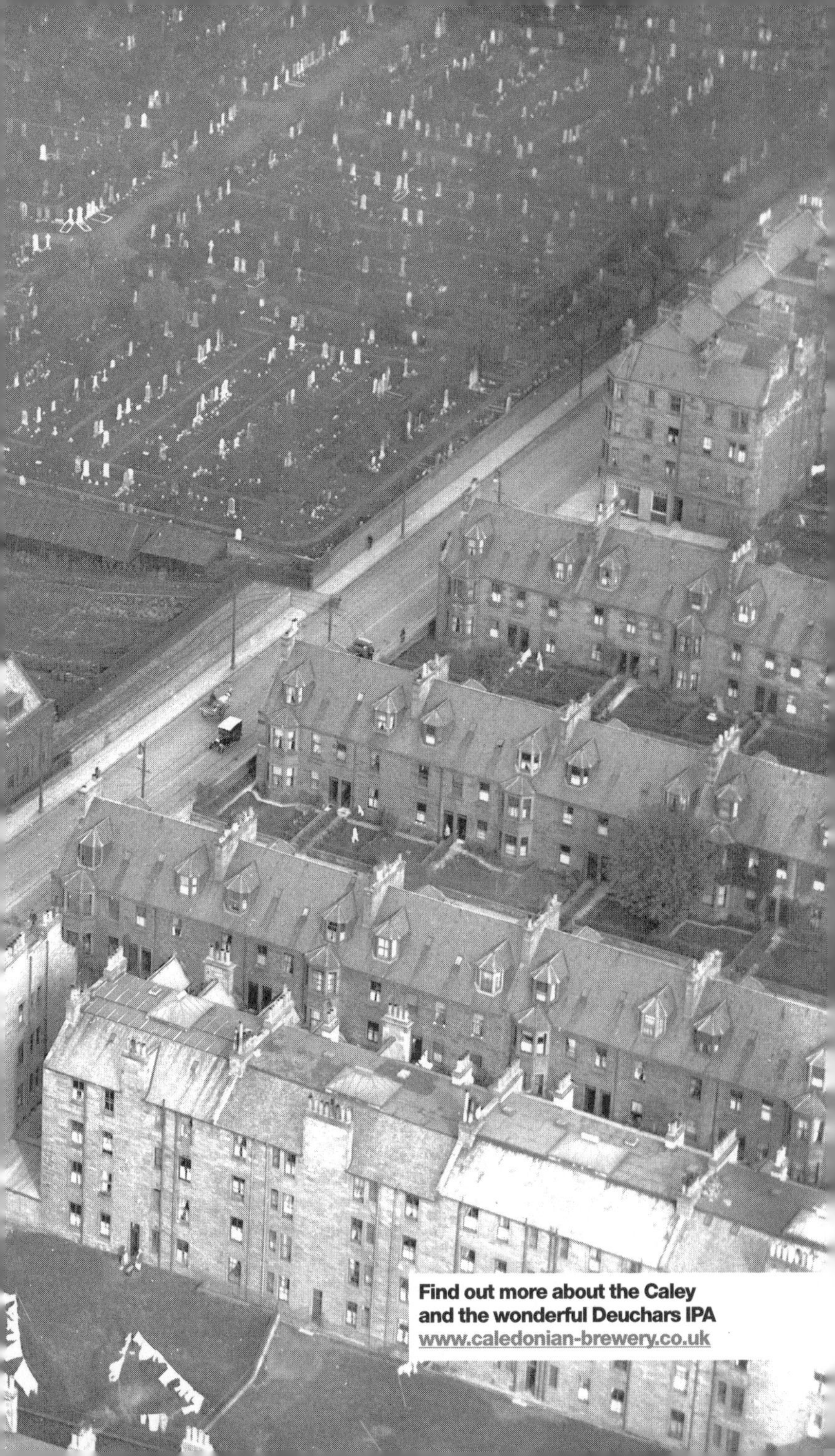

Yet Edinburgh and the surrounding towns and villages were never going to generate sufficient demand on their own. What opened the world to the city's brewers was India Pale Ale or IPA. A combination of hard water and plenty of hops gave the city a house style that was lower in strength and lighter in colour than beers brewed further west. Breweries around Glasgow used softer water and generally lower quality hops and malt to produce much darker ales and stouts. They could be highly alcoholic and were sometimes blackened with liquorice or wormwood to resemble Guinness, which brought a taste of home to the city's large Irish community.

The beer in Edinburgh took less time to produce, which pleased the brewers and, thanks to the magic ingredient of gypsum, seemed to travel well. Its fame spread south of the border and eventually to the fringes of the British Empire. As its name implies, India Pale Ale was originally created for export, being a robust, thirst-quenching beer that could withstand the long voyage by sea. It just so happened that it became extremely popular in the north of England. Not all of it came from Edinburgh, but a sizeable proportion did.

From the mid-19th century onwards the city's brewers began to spread out from the centre to colonise outlying sites within the 'charmed circle' of brewing wells, particularly Craigmillar on the south side. To the west there was William McEwan's mighty Fountain Brewery, and the rather smaller Caledonian Brewery in Slateford a mile or so beyond. Both benefited from good transport links with sidings to the Caledonian Railway and access to the Union Canal, which ran from Edinburgh to Glasgow.

Those breweries still left in the Old Town remained a remarkably long time despite their cramped conditions. The Canongate, which still had seven breweries as late as the 1940s, had been home to William Younger's brewing empire since 1777. Having merged with McEwan's to form what became Scottish & Newcastle, the company's Holyrood brewery remained at the foot of the Canongate until it closed in 1986. It was bulldozed into history along with its neighbour – the Abbey Brewery, which was flattened to make room for the new Scottish Parliament in the mid-1990s.

By the 19th century, brewing was at its peak and Edinburgh was one of the foremost brewing centres in the United Kingdom. Some 41 breweries thrived in the city, all benefiting from the plentiful supply of local barley and good quality water drawn from Edinburgh's 'charmed circle'.

The story of brewing in the 20th century is one of endless contraction as breweries were swallowed up, closed down or merged to form ever-larger units. While it happened throughout Britain it was all the more poignant in Edinburgh because so many great breweries bit the dust. When the last drop of beer dribbled out of the massive Fountain Brewery in 2004 it really did feel like the end of an era. And yet as the eight-acre site fell silent awaiting re-development into an 'urban village' of shops and housing, it was not quite the end. Before the papers could print the final obituary of an industry that has been part of the city for over eight centuries, there was still one small brewery left. The beer barons of the past would have found this hard to believe, but if asked to pick which lone outpost would manage to cling on – few if any would have guessed correctly. Despite the perennial threat of closure, the wholesale consolidation of brewing and the odd fire, the Caledonian Brewery has survived against all odds. It is a remarkable story.

The Caley

The Caledonian Brewery, Edinburgh's last remaining brewery was opened by George Lorimer Jr in 1869. It was the result of two things: the death of his father and his love of the golf course… On the afternoon of 13th January 1865, oil lamps at Edinburgh's Theatre Royal set the props alight. By the time George Lorimer Snr was walking past, the wind had fanned the fire into a blaze. A labourer had been crushed in the vestry of St Mary's Catholic Church next door and Lorimer rushed in to save him. Minutes later the entire north wall of the theatre fell, collapsing the church and burying both men. Like the opening of a Rebus novel, this event was to have widespread repercussions.

Lorimer Snr, a successful building contractor, was well known as the city's Lord Dean of Guild and his heroic death was widely reported. His son George was a keen golfer and member of the Bruntsfield Links Golfing Society, which met at the Golf Tavern, the oldest surviving clubhouse in the world. Many of Edinburgh's leading brewers were members and at some point the young George met Robert Clark, the head brewer at the Alexander Melvin brewery. The two became friends and began to discuss a possible venture. Scottish beer was booming at the time with production at over a million barrels in 1865, having doubled in eight years.

On his 21st birthday in 1868, George inherited the family fortune and in the following year Lorimer & Clark's Caledonian Brewery was founded on Slateford Road, then on the western fringes of the city. It was just within the famed 'charmed circle' – or underground lake that is full of pure, pristine water perfect for making beer. A borehole was sunk (which still supplies the brewery's water to this day) to 200 metres below the surface. The Caley also took advantage of the new railway line and had its own siding to offload the hops and barley. The empty casks would also arrive by rail to be sent back full of beer.

Under George Lorimer, who ran the business until he died in 1919, the Caley (as it became known) produced a range of beers and stouts and sold them all over Scotland. The main brand was 'Lorimer's Best Scotch', which like other local beers, did particularly well in the north-east of England. It seems the clean, well-hopped taste of the pale ales traditionally brewed in Edinburgh was ideal for cutting through the dust and grime in people's throats after a hard day's digging coal or building ships. The brand's popularity was noticed by the Sunderland-based brewer Vaux, who bought into the business in 1919. After the Second World War, Vaux led the English invasion of Scotland's breweries. Having

gained full control of the Caley in 1947, it went on to acquire a string of others including Usher's Park Brewery in 1960.

By this stage, virtually the entire production at the Caley was going into Lorimer's Best Scotch, which was trucked down the A1 to quench an insatiable thirst among Geordies. Meanwhile, moving in the opposite direction was a much larger quantity of McEwan's Export, tankered north from Newcastle to the canning factory in Scotland. With such anomalies common, rationalisation of Britain's brewing industry was inevitable. For the Caley, a small and largely overlooked asset in Vaux's portfolio, the future appeared grim.

In the mid-80s demand was almost entirely for big brands of keg beer and lager, which Lorimer & Clark's little brewery was completely ill-equipped to supply. Eventually in 1986, Vaux decided to concentrate brewing locally in Sunderland, and announced its decision to cease brewing in Edinburgh. It looked like the end of the road, and probably at any other time in any other city, it would have been. Compared to the vast Fountain Brewery down the road, the Caley looked like a throwback to a bygone age, an anachronism waiting for the bulldozer. Perhaps if it hadn't been built of brick, which meant the building was listed, it would now be a car park or supermarket. However, just at this time, there were signs that the tide was beginning to turn, at least in Edinburgh, with just enough publicans prepared to support cask ale.

In 1987, sensing there was a real opportunity, the management engineered a buy-out of the brewery. Also being a little further out helped its survival: there was less pressure from developers than there was around Holyrood. Certainly no one ever proposed building the new Scottish Parliament on Slateford Road! But it was not new ownership that saved the brewery, but the creation of a hugely popular beer a few years later. Without Deuchars there would definitely be no Caley.

Deuchars

The inspiration for Deuchars came from the past, beers such as McLaughlin's Heavy and Campbell Hope & King's IPA. It needed to be light, thirst quenching and well-hopped. Not something deep and murky, but clean and brass-bright that might even seduce someone who had only ever drunk lager.

Robert Deuchars was an old brewing dynasty split between Tyne & Wear and Edinburgh, where its Duddingston brewery was one of 41 operating in the city in 1900. Like all but the Caley, it was demolished years ago. At some point in the 1980s, Head Brewer Russell Sharp found himself in his favourite pub, the Canny Man's, discussing a possible new beer with his friend Ian White who created the Bow Bar. After a good few pints, Russell stumbled off to the gents and came face to face with an old beer label stuck to the wall. As luck would have it, the label declared 'Deuchars'. A quick check revealed that the original trademark had lapsed, and thus a new ale was born. Compared to all the brainstorming and test marketing usually associated with a new product launch, this makes a far better story. Slowly Deuchars IPA caught on, and it spread throughout its home city to pubs across the UK, grabbing a fistful of awards en route, most notably CAMRA's (Campaign for Real Ale) 'Supreme Champion Beer of Britain' in 2002 and Best Cask Ale at the Brewing Industry International Awards in 2005.

When Ian Rankin first came to Edinburgh as a student in 1978, he drank the heavier beers on offer from the Caley, but switched to Deuchars IPA soon after its launch... as did his fictional creation Inspector Rebus: 'I've tasted a multitude of beers and lagers in over a dozen countries, but nothing quite matches Deuchars,' Ian recently commented. I don't think I've ever had a bad pint of the stuff. Refined and creamy, it manages to provide plenty of flavour without sledgehammer amounts of alcohol... When I'm away on tour with my books, it's one of the things I miss most. It always gives me great pleasure when Rebus fans from as far afield as New Zealand and Canada wander into the Oxford Bar and decide to order a helping of Deuchars. They always seem to enjoy it...so much so that one often proves not to be enough, and they find themselves an hour or two later having made friends for life of the regulars and staff, and with memories of good company and good beer to take back home with them.'

Which brings us on to the subject of Edinburgh pubs ...

EDINBURGH PUBS: A BRIEF HISTORY

'There is nothing which has yet been contrived by man, by which so much happiness is produced as by a good tavern or inn' declared Dr Johnson.

He could well have been talking about Edinburgh, which has always had a wealth of great bars and pubs. The fact this is still true today has been the inspiration for this little book. But more than that, it was what inspired the creation of Deuchars in the first place. The Caledonian Brewery deliberately set out to create a beer that its home city could be proud of. Yet this is all quite recent compared to the long, convoluted history of the Edinburgh pub.

As soon as people began brewing their own beer they began selling it on the premises in a kitchen or parlour. These gradually became the licensed taverns that popped up all over Edinburgh. Given the crowded confines of the city perched on its narrow ridge – the Royal Mile – they became particularly important here. They offered people an escape from cramped dwellings, a place to drink, gossip, do business, gamble and chase women. In general they reflected the classless nature of the Old Town where everyone lived cheek by jowl.

That said, taverns came in all shapes and sizes from the most Spartan and evil-smelling dive full of the city's lowlife to places of some sophistication like Fortune's Tavern – a favourite of Edinburgh's high society. Enlightenment figures like Smith, Hume, Ferguson and Burns frequented John Downie's Tavern, which survived until 1835 when it was knocked down to make room for the George IV Bridge. It was famous for its rabbit warren of mainly windowless rooms of which 'the coffin' was little more than a closet. It was also famed for its beer – Archibald Younger's Edinburgh Ale, with its notable strength and ability to glue the drinker's lips together.

Particular bars were associated with Edinburgh's clubs like the Anchor Tavern

and the Crollachan Fencibles of which Burns was a member. Among the myriad of other examples were the Cape Club, the Marrow Bone Club and the Poker Club which eventually became the New Club. There was also the Spendthrift Club whose members were not allowed to spend more than four pennies on a night's entertainment and the Sweating Club who chased anyone they met until they perspired – a sort of 18th century take on 'happy slapping' perhaps? Certain bars were also associated with particular professions. Lawyers and physicians favoured the Star & Garter in Writer's Court, though if you came seeking legal advice it could often be hard to find anyone sober. In his *Traditions of Edinburgh*, Robert Chambers wrote of judges 'reeling home from a close in the High Street,' and then later on in court, 'mounting the bench... in a crapulous state.' Depending on taste and income, people drank claret, ale and porter, which was first brewed in Glasgow in the 1770s and soon became popular in Edinburgh to drink with oysters harvested along the Firth of Forth, particularly around Mussleburgh. Oyster bars had become hugely fashionable by the end of the 18th century, especially around the Cowgate. In theory taverns closed at the sound of the 10 o'clock drum, though in practice many stayed open. The drum also signalled that most feared of the city's street cries – 'Gardy-loo!' – a warning that a shower of filth was about to rain down from on high as residents emptied their chamber pots into the street.

The conviviality of tavern life reflected the city's remarkable social mix. But it was not to last. In 1767 the young architect James Craig submitted plans to build a New Town on land north of the Castle. In contrast to the ramshackle tenements and dark, fetid closes this was to be a monument to symmetrical purity. Six years later, the North Bridge was erected to connect the Royal Mile to the Promised Land beyond. Those with means could scarcely wait to swap the claustrophobic Old Town for the spacious Georgian splendour of the New. Edinburgh was never the same again.

In 1822 there were 28 registered brewers in Edinburgh. By 1841 that number had rocketed to 193. Most worked on a small scale supplying a very local market, but the increase was indicative of the city's rising population and its growing thirst for beer. Inevitably, rising consumption led to increasing concern and the birth of the temperance movement. From a first outpost in Greenock in 1829, Temperance societies spread like a rash across Scotland preaching moderation and more tax. Visiting campaigners like Father Theobald Matthew from Ireland urged Scots to join the two million Irish who had already signed the pledge. Some of his most strident supporters claimed that habitual drunkards risked 'spontaneous combustion'! In Edinburgh the authorities began closing 'superfluous dram shops', there were over 500 licensed premises – the vast majority of them in the Old Town. Much of the New Town was a pub-free zone apart from Rose Street which had 32 bars in 1846.

South of the border, urban pubs were being forced to smarten up and compete with neighbouring shops. They adopted gas lamps and plate glass windows to become the early gin palaces whose appeal is explained by Peter Haydon in his book, *Beer & Britannia*, 'In the days before street lighting, the appearance of the gin palace would have been like a beacon in the darkness for the miserable poor who thronged their doors.' The same makeover spread north to Edinburgh in the latter half of the 19th century transforming simple taverns into glittering palaces for the people. The drink, though, was not gin, but beer and later whisky.

Originally pubs were open from six in the morning until midnight apart from during church services on Sundays. There were also plenty of illicit dram shops, open all hours, and grocers who used to serve drinks over the counter until forbidden by the Forbes Mackenzie Act of 1853. Under the Act, pubs had to shut at 11pm and on the sabbath when drinkers took refuge in hotel bars and shebeens. From then on, the authorities increasingly sought to limit people's access to booze by restricting licences and opening hours. Not that it had much effect on the amount consumed, just the speed at which it was drunk.

This pleased the publican and brewer by reducing competition and overheads, as much as the temperance lobby whose one time battle-cry was; 'we must make drink stink'. As for the man in the street, no-one bothered to ask whether he liked being packed like a sardine in a tin, unable to sit and forced to drink against the clock. Inevitably the media played its part in demonising Scottish boozers filled with losers on a fast-track to oblivion. 'Not in the worst dens of New York can a more brutalised crowd be witnessed. Bareheaded and barefooted women with infants in their arms, uncouth Magdalenes scarred with the leprosy of sin, men on the borderland of delirium tremens. . .' thundered an editorial in 1892 in the *North British Daily Mail*. (Some things never change.)

Yet while the bad side of Scottish drinking culture could be very bad indeed, there was a much more civilised side as well. Despite the anti-drink lobby and local councils who seemed innately suspicious of anyone having a good time, Scotland's leading city pubs entered a golden age in late Victorian times. With their expanse of polished wood, elaborate pillars and moulded ceilings, these were temples of design. There was a real pride in craftsmanship as each bar sought to compete with its rival across the street and attract the city's floating drinkers. Light from gas lamps bounced off brass fittings and walls of mirrors, etched glass and ceramic tiles to create a sparkling interior far brighter than most people's homes. The focal point was the bar itself, which was often moved into the centre to help speed up service and placate the licensing authorities. The old-style howff with its rabbit warren of snugs and bars was frowned upon. Who knew what mischief the masses might get up to if left unsupervised? It was far better to have one large room with an island bar where the publican could keep an eye on his flock like a parson in his pulpit. By coincidence some Edinburgh architects who specialised in pubs also designed churches, and by employing the same joiners the design could be quite similar.

Behind the bar, on an elaborately carved gantry, would be casks of wine, sherry and above all whisky. Often this was blended by the landlord himself, who sold it by the jug as well as by the dram. Some would go further and develop a wholesale business for their house blend. Licensed grocers would do the same, and sometimes these became huge brands like Chivas Regal in Aberdeen and Famous Grouse in Perth.

In the transition between the rustic Old Town howff and the glittering late Victorian bar, drinking in Edinburgh may have lost some of its humanity, yet the city's pubs have maintained their individuality and provide the same egalitarian space today. Then as now, what really makes a pub are the people who are found within its walls – from those behind the bar to the regulars gathered round it. And while a lot of old pubs have gone or been changed out of recognition, a surprising number have survived perhaps more in Edinburgh than any other city in Britain. They have been joined by some great, more recent pubs, full of warmth and character.

Over the years the Edinburgh pub has been endlessly converted, flattened, knocked about and rebuilt. People speculated about its future as they always have. Would every bar become an Identikit theme-pub? Would pub culture be washed away in a tide of fizzy lager and Tartan Special? Well it hasn't happened yet, and from what one can tell, it won't for some time. Here in Edinburgh good beer and good pubs have prevailed. Long may it last.

REBUS & RANKIN – DOWN THE PUB

Right from the start of the Rebus series, from about the fourth page of *Knots & Crosses* (the first Rebus novel) you're in a pub.

Inspector Rebus and Edinburgh pubs go together like politicians and expense accounts. It's hard to imagine the one without the other. To bestselling author Ian Rankin, a pub is the perfect location for a writer: it's more than a place to slake your thirst, it's also a fascinating social 'laboratory' that mixes people from different backgrounds, different jobs and different attitudes over that most egalitarian of drinks – the pint of beer. For Rankin, a pub can be a refuge from the world, a place of good conversation, democratic spirit, a few laughs, relaxation, and community. It's also a great literary device where the characters of a novel can mingle with impunity – pubs are great levellers. A pub is also the perfect place for a cop like Detective John Rebus. He can overhear stories from colleagues and criminals alike: who hasn't let off steam in a pub at the end of a long day? If a villain can't be found, then someone with the inside gen could loosen his tongue after a few pints… Remember, when Rebus meets an informant in a pub, he's carrying on a grand old Edinburgh tradition – using the pub as a place of work. There was a time in Edinburgh's history when, if you wanted to see a lawyer, you went to a pub. The lawyer who didn't have an office staked out a corner in a pub, where he would sit and work and clients would come in and meet him. It's a tradition authors like Ian maintain to this day.

The British pub culture is pretty well unique: pubs are the focal points of a community – their social hub, and home for some. And it's the same in the Rebus novels: the reticent Detective Inspector Rebus uses his local as a surrogate home. He goes there to think, to escape and to drown his sorrows: he drinks alone, confronting his own personal demons and he drinks despite his work, not

because of it. And he generally drinks his pint of Deuchars IPA in the Oxford Bar.

Ian has been drinking in Edinburgh's Oxford Bar since 1984, when his flatmate was the part-time barman. Tucked away down a narrow lane in the city centre, it seemed to represent the 'hidden Edinburgh' that Ian was trying to write about. Despite changing ownership and its (now) worldwide fame as Rebus's local, the seedy charm of the pub hasn't changed in over 100 years – it would take more than a spot of notoriety to change the Oxford Bar. The minute you walk over the 'emergency entrance', there's a democracy at work. As long as you've got money in your pocket for a drink, you're the same as everybody else. Early in the Rebus novels, Rankin decided to make it Inspector John Rebus's local as well as his own; then and now, the detective favoured the same tipple as his creator, namely Deuchar's IPA.

Even when Rebus is on the wagon – as in *The Hanging Garden* he's a pub regular: 'He thought of the Oxford Bar. Even on the wagon, he'd stayed a regular, drinking cola and mugs of coffee. A pub like the Ox was about so much more than just the hooch. It was therapy and refuge, entertainment and art. He checked his watch, thinking he could head down there now. Just a couple of whiskies and a beer, something to make him feel good about himself until the morning. The phone rang again. He picked it up. "Evening, John." Rebus smiled, leaned back in his chair. "Jack, you must be a bloody mind reader..."'

Does anyone fancy a pint...?

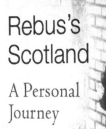

IAN RANKIN

Rebus's Scotland

A Personal
Journey

PHOTOGRAPHED BY
Tricia **Malley** and
Ross **Gillespie**

THROUGH A GLASS DARKLY

The Scottish TV comedy show *Chewing the Fat* features a recurring sketch where a reluctant toper is urged to 'take a drink'. The community around him will not be appeased until he indulges, like them, in alcohol. This goes deep into the psyche of the Scot. We bond in drink, throw off our customary reticence, and are suspicious of non-subscribers.

I was probably eleven or twelve when a New Year visitor to our house, maybe not out of his teens himself, tried to persuade me to take an illicit swig from his bottle of whisky. He was confident I would crave that forbidden taste. The thing was, he was years too late. Neither of my parents was a great drinker, but a bottle of whisky was kept in the pantry for visitors (there was probably a bottle of sherry in there, too). When I was eight or nine, I would sneak into the pantry and take the occasional sip – never very much, but eventually the level in the bottle fell to the extent that my father came to my bedroom one night to ask if I was the culprit. I readily admitted the crime. I had 'prior' after all: my parents saved sixpences in an empty Dimple whisky bottle, and I had gone through a phase of stealing these and leaving them dotted around the house. My dad gave me a good talking to on both occasions, and also started marking the label of the whisky bottle.

During the 1960s, he had brought home treasures from the grocer's shop. On the window-ledge in my bedroom stood a handsome collection of promotional items, including a porcelain white horse (advertising White Horse whisky) and a foot-high, detailed statue of Mr Johnnie Walker himself, complete with top hat, walking-cane and monocle. Is it any wonder I wanted to taste this stuff that dreams were made of? (My dad also brought boxes of chocolate biscuits home, but that's another story.)

Friday nights were when my dad went out with his cronies. For a while, I insisted that he visit my bedroom on his return, so I could check he wasn't drunk. Why I did this I've no idea. I probably saw my father drunk on only half a dozen occasions, face merry, lacking any bluster or belligerence. These were usually family affairs: New Year gatherings and weddings. My own rite of passage came when I was seventeen. That Hogmanay, I had my own New Year's bottle (Southern Comfort). Bars had started serving me the previous year; I don't recall ever being turned away or asked for proof of age. On a school trip to Switzerland, some of us had managed to buy duty free booze on board the ferry. Our teacher discovered this and made us promise to hide it away in our hotel room and take it home with us unopened. She relented, however, on the final night of our stay, and came to our room for a snifter, leaving soon after in less sanguine mood when we admitted we'd already necked the lot . . .

I had one aunt who lived near us and drank only cherry brandy, insisting it was not alcoholic. Another aunt always seemed very quiet and mousy to me, but came out of her shell at one wedding reception when, after a few too many Sweetheart stouts, she helped me treat the company to a skittish rendition of 'There's a Hole in My Bucket'. Near the start of *The Falls*, Rebus is at Farmer Watson's retirement party when a fellow detective, Bobby Hogan, suggests that the pair of them regale the company with this same song. This is shortly before Rebus, in his cups by now, gets into trouble by turning up at the home of a missing teenager . . .

Rebus has had a problem with drink from the word go. I was probably thinking of all those American private eye films, the bottle of bourbon brought out to freshen a client's glass. And Rebus had a good reason to drink: there were things in his past he needed to forget. In *Knots & Crosses*, booze sees him stagger into bed with a female inebriate, whom he nearly attacks. Later on, in *Dead Souls*, Farmer Watson prepares for a funeral by pouring two stiff drinks:

> Rebus nodded, watching the man pour. Cascading sound of mountain streams. Usquebaugh in the Gaelic. Uisge: water; beatha: life. Water of life. Beatha sounding like 'birth'. Each drink was a birth to Rebus's mind. But as his doctor kept telling him, each drop was a little death, too.

Some of my favourite descriptions in the books involve bars and the people who drink in them:

> Old men sat with their half-pint glasses, staring emptily towards the front door. Were they wondering what was outside? Or were they just scared that whatever was out there would one day force its way in?

> He'd quietened down, gone all sulky in a corner, standing there with head bent under the weight of a cigarette. The pint glass seemed heavy, too, so that his wrist sagged beneath it, beer dripping down on to his shoes and the wooden floor.

The first of these quotations comes from *Knots & Crosses*, written between the ages of twenty-four and twenty-five. It shows that its young author was well acquainted with traditional drinking dens, and with the reasons why his jaded elders might frequent them. A pub, at its best, is a place of safety, a retreat from the world. It offers sanctuary, comedy, space for reflection, and the makings of a hangover. It's a place to meet people, or to be alone; a place of vivid conversation or silent reflection. Some of my favourites have been swept away – knocked down in some cases, or changing hands and being transformed into 'style bars'. The character of a bar has much to do with its clientele, but that clientele can be fickle, and changes to the fabric of the bar can cause them to head elsewhere.

In the sleeve notes to some of his albums, singer-songwriter Jackie Leven usually acknowledges a debt to bars which have sustained him through touring and writing. Most of these are real, though I'm doubtful of the veracity of the 'Fuckin Bastard' in Dundee, to give one example. In similar vein, I began the Rebus series writing about semi-fictitious bars with names such as the Sutherland. However, I'd also started drinking at the Oxford Bar, a small and wilfully 'clubby' place not far from Princes Street, yet so wonderfully hidden away that strangers seldom stumbled upon it. One of the students I was sharing a flat with was a regular there (and part-time barman). By my second or third visit, the other bar staff could pour my choice of beer unprompted. I was busy meantime making friends, and discovering that among the clientele were a number of serving and retired police officers.

Perfect.

The Oxford Bar was first identified by name in *Mortal Causes.* Rebus liked its atmosphere and the fact that it sold 'quarter gills' (ie: larger measures of spirits than in most pubs). Even when he stops drinking for a time, however, as happens in *The Hanging Garden*, he continues to haunt the place:

A pub like the Ox was about so much more than just the hooch. It was therapy and refuge, entertainment and art.

By this stage in the life of the series, I'd decided to use real locations as much as possible, and this extended to the characters themselves. Harry, mentioned in the books as 'Edinburgh's rudest barman . . . quite a feat, considering the competition', really was the barman at the Ox (he now owns the place, and is only rude to a choice few of us who've known him for some time). In *Resurrection Men* I even make reference to Willie Ross, who was the real-life owner of the place a few decades back, and in *Set in Darkness* I make use of a number of real drinkers, too, including Muir, Hayden and Gordon (first names only, to protect the guilty), plus other real bars I've been known to frequent, such as the Maltings and Swany's.

This helps give the books a sense of verisimilitude, plus it's easier for me than having to make places up.

By the time I reached high school, there was a culture of drinking at break-times. Boys would take it in turns to bring a 'mixture' in their satchel. This comprised any kind of container – including on at least one occasion an unwashed ketchup bottle – filled with a mix of decanted spirits from the parental drinks cabinet. A good 'mixture' might be unequal parts dark rum, gin, vodka, whisky and crème de menthe. The container would be passed around until empty. One of my friends keeled over in the chemistry lab after a lunchtime session, but this was put down to heat-stroke, fortunately for the rest of us.

School discos and Christmas dances would be preceded by a few tipples in the cemetery – usually Woodpecker cider, cans of Special Brew, and vodka diluted with some sweetened orange juice (this last a forerunner of today's

alcopops). The occasions made us garrulous and brotherly.
And angry.
And ill.

One night, after a session at a friend's house, I stumbled home drunk, tried to make my way upstairs to the toilet, but was found by my mother just as my gorge started to rise. Another scolding.

My background is Rebus's, therefore he probably shared at least a few of my underage adventures. But he left school at fifteen and joined the Army – with its macho culture fuelled, in part, by prodigious intake of alcohol. Maybe his serious drinking started there; or maybe it's his Scottishness that makes him 'take a drink', even when he doesn't really feel like one. During his short period of abstinence (between *Black & Blue* and *The Hanging Garden*) he carried with him a bottle of the hard stuff – a little 'grenade' of sorts. And it was this grenade he turned to when forced to face the fact of his daughter's hit-and-run.

So is drink a lazy substitute for Rebus? A way of dealing with problems and stresses? If so, then he's to all intents an alcoholic, but I think his relationship to alcohol is slightly more complex:

> One of the reasons Rebus drank was to put him to sleep. He had trouble sleeping when sober. He'd stare into the darkness, willing it to form shapes so that he might better understand it. He'd try to make sense of life – his early disastrous Army years; his failed marriage; his failings as father, friend, lover – and end up in tears. And if he did eventually stumble into sober sleep, there would be troubled dreams, dreams about ageing and dying, decay and blight . . . Drunk, his sleep was dreamless, or seemed that way on waking *(Let It Bleed)*.

The word for this is 'maudlin', but it reflects a potential problem in many of us. There are millions of people out there who drink to excess at the end of the working week in order to blot out the memories of that same week. Stressed professionals lock the door behind them and reach for the corkscrew or the gin. Rebus is no different, except that he is not a social drinker. Even when in company, he's not really of the company. He's always alone with his thoughts and his personal demons, and he drinks despite his work, not because of it:

> Police routine gave his daily life its only shape and substance; it gave him a schedule to work to, a reason to get up in the morning. He loathed his free time, dreaded Sundays off. He lived to work, and in a very real sense he worked to live, too: the much-maligned Protestant work ethic. Subtract work from the equation and the day became flabby, like releasing jelly from its mould. Besides, without work, what reason had he not to drink *(Let It Bleed)*?

In *Scottish Journey*, Edwin Muir sums up the national attitude to alcohol in this way: 'Scottish people drink spasmodically and intensely, for the sake of a momentary but complete release, whereas the English like to bathe and paddle about bucolically in a mild puddle of beer.'

Several things strike me about this. One is that Muir is describing the Scots very much as binge-drinkers. Another is that he could just as easily be describing an addiction to hard drugs ('a momentary but complete release'), as portrayed in novels such as the Edinburgh-based *Trainspotting*. Thirdly, were he alive today and visiting any town of size in England on a Friday night, he might wish to revise his opinion of that 'mild puddle'. In retreading Muir's steps half a century later, James Campbell mentions 'the monotonous peacefulness common to all Scottish small towns, which in the evening turns to eerie silence, punctuated by the sounds of children and drunks'.

Nowadays, however, the drunks themselves are likely to be children, their punctuations replacing any trace of silence. Yet while our cities' night-time streets are alive with drunks, I see little obvious drunkenness in places like the Oxford Bar. It seems to have its own unwritten rules, and somehow these are obeyed. The government-sanctioned phrase 'Drink Responsibly' might have been thought up after a quiet session in the back room of the Ox. I've only once encountered violence over its threshold (and that ruck involved journalists, for whom no rules are sacred). The same can be said for the other bars I've been known to visit throughout Scotland. My favourite in Glasgow is the Horseshoe:

> It was central and crowded with people who took their drinking seriously, the kind of place where no one looked askance at a tea-stained shirt, so long as the wearer had about him the price of his drink. Rebus knew immediately that it would be a place of rules and rituals, a place where regulars would know from the moment they walked through the door that their drink of preference was already being poured for them *(Resurrection Men)*.

I could just as well be describing the Oxford Bar.

My only rule in choosing these watering-holes has been: never drink in a bar with bouncers on the door. If they're expecting trouble, trouble is probably on its way.

Aggression and alcohol go fist in hand, of course, and there's something in the Scottish psyche that makes us prone to dark thoughts when drunk, and occasionally dark deeds, too. One of the theories of *Dr Jekyll and Mr Hyde* (that most Edinburgh of novels, yet infuriatingly set in London) is that it refers to its author's drunken exploits in the stews of his native city. Robert Louis Stevenson was born into a respectable professional family, and lived in what remains one of the finest streets in Edinburgh, yet as a young man he was hungry to explore another side of his character, a side unleashed during visits to the rough-houses in the chaotic maze of the Old Town (he himself lived in the rational and well-ordered 'New Town'). One of the frontispieces to this current book shows Stevenson's exaggerated version of the Edinburgh he knew. He's describing the worsening condition of the Old Town, the encroaching 'sordidness' and lawlessness bringing policemen to the scene.

To this day alcohol remains one of the main generators of 'domestic crime', a world away from the distillery tours enjoyed by Iain Banks in his travel book *Raw Spirit*. (Banks's choice of title, as usual, has a double meaning: he discusses the raw spirit of the Scots along the way.)

The rich relationship between the Scots and alcohol goes beyond our invention of whisky, and drips down into the language. We possess myriad words for drunkenness: hoolit, steaming, guttered, wellied, blootered. The word 'mingin' was current in Scotland well before it entered the lexicon south of the border. We call alcohol 'bevvy', short for 'beverage', turning it into a euphemism. We go to the pub for a 'wee swallie' (a small swallow). The pub culture of the British Isles is pretty well unique. Pubs are our social clubs. A good 'local' may include its own darts team or quiz team. Golf tournaments may be organised, along with trips abroad for rugby matches. The landlord stands each and every regular a free drink at New Year, and when those same regulars head off on holiday, they send postcards which are displayed behind the bar. In this way, the pub becomes a surrogate home, its drinkers a kind of family – dysfunctional, to be sure, but tight-knit.

This is another reason why Rebus drinks. He has no family around him, and precious few friends. Bars suit that side of the Scottish character which is reticent and introverted. They're places where you can be as invisible as you like. At the same time, they are also confessionals. I've had near-strangers tell me their innermost secrets after one too many drinks. They say it can be easier to talk to strangers than to one's own close family, and this seems to be the case. Of course, not all bars offer similar comforts. In Glasgow, there are Rangers pubs and Celtic pubs, and the unwitting visitor must be careful not to make the wrong choice. Drinkers in most places are territorial anyway, wary of the new face. You could be an undercover cop or a social security spy. I once walked into a bar in Uig on the Isle of Skye, and the change in atmosphere was immediate and unsettling. If someone had been playing the piano, they would have ceased. In my memory, the barman was drying pint-glasses with a towel, like a scene from a cowboy film. When I asked for Talisker, the local malt, the murmur of conversation started up again. I'd selected the correct password.

It probably was little different in Stevenson's day. Many of the scenes I describe in my books seem to me timeless. Here's Rebus, encountering Cafferty late one night in the Royal Oak, a bar renowned for its live music. Cafferty is regaling the place with a rendition of a Burns song:

One of the barmaids took Rebus's order: a half of Eighty and a whisky. There was no conversation in the bar, respectful silence and even a tear in one patriot's eye as she sat on her stool with her brandy and Coke raised to her lips, her ragged boyfriend stroking her shoulders from behind. When the song finished, there was applause, a few whistles and cheers. Cafferty bowed his head, lifted his whisky glass and toasted the room. As the clapping subsided, the accordionist took it as his cue to commence.' *(Set in Darkness)*

This is a Scotland Stevenson would surely recognise – maudlin to a degree (that tearful 'patriot'), democratic in its respect of anyone's right to sing a song, and with an acknowledgement of the ephemeral nature of existence (the way Cafferty's singing melts into the next musical act). In centuries past, Scotland's 'howffs' and oyster bars were places where the rich and poor could mingle – something not possible in the hierarchical world outside. Poets, ruffians and harlots could be found there. The poet Robert Fergusson wrote with almost filmic quality of Edinburgh's low life in the eighteenth century, a time when thirty million oysters a year would be taken from the Forth estuary to accompany the citizens' various tipples. These bars were ideal locations for cops. If the culprit couldn't be found there, someone with some inside gen might be persuaded to talk over a free drink. Writers share some similarities with detectives: we have questions about the world that need answering; we look to our fellow humans, seeking motives and wondering about their secret lives. And like detectives, writers have always enjoyed the drinking life, bars our private studies. We find characters there, and stories, and themes. We covet anecdotes and linguistic gems. The best pubs show us Scotland in miniature, with all its uncertainties, problems and joie de vivre.

As I write, there are moves by the Scottish Executive towards an outright ban on smoking in bars, clubs and restaurants. If alcohol has taken its toll on the Scots, then so have cigarettes. When a similar ban was imposed in Ireland, it was said it would never work. Scotland's First Minister, however, was energised after a visit to Dublin. In many pubs in Scotland, a pint and a 'fag' go hand in hand (as it were). In the early novels, Rebus is trying to rein in his nicotine consumption, aware that he is killing himself by degrees. By the later novels, however, his cravings have the better of him. I grew up with two parents who smoked into their fifties. Both eventually gave up, and maybe Rebus can be persuaded to do the same. Otherwise, he will have to step out of the warm, well-lit Oxford Bar and into the inhospitable Edinburgh night for his regular fix.

I prefaced my novel *Let It Bleed* with a quotation from Martin Amis's *Money*: 'Without women, life is a pub.' Hard to tell if Amis's narrator thinks this a good thing; John Rebus certainly finds his local howff a suitable alternative.

Just one more small part of his failing.

(Taken from *Rebus's Scotland* by Ian Rankin © John Rebus Ltd)

THE NEW TOWN

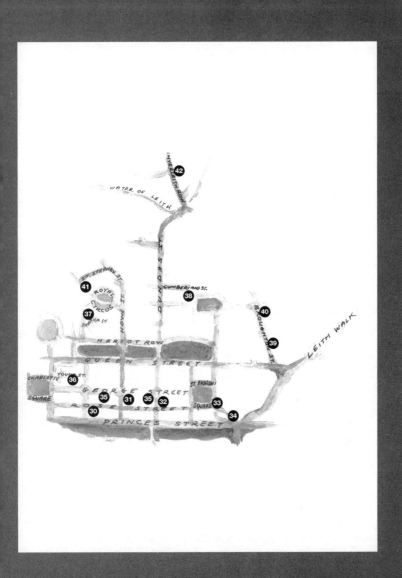

THE KENILWORTH
152 ROSE STREET EH2 4AZ

Like the covers of a book, Sir Walter Scott has Rose Street neatly bound between the Abbotsford and the Kenilworth. Both pubs date from the 1890s and were originally owned by a wine and spirits merchant called Peter Fisher. The former was named after the writer's house in the borders, while *Kenilworth* is one of his 'Waverley novels' published anonymously in 1824. Scott was a prolific novelist, poet, critic and biographer whose works remained international best-sellers long after his death. Yet Sir Walter's influence on Scotland went way beyond literature. He, more than anyone else, helped brand an entire nation with his romantic vision and made life there imitate his art.

In his honour the Victorians named the capital's main railway station Waverley and had the Scott Monument erected just outside in 1846. In it the great man sits brooding surrounded by a towering edifice of blackened sandstone – described by some as a Gothic take on the Thunderbird Five rocket. From here it is a short walk to Rose Street, which was originally built to house some of the craftsmen who had helped build the New Town in the late 18th century. By the time Peter Fisher opened the Kenilworth in 1893, Rose Street had been transformed into an oasis of drink. It grew this way because of demand in a distinctly dry area. The public façade of the New Town with its wide avenues and sweeping crescents was all about classical elegance whose purity could never be defiled by anything as raucous as a pub. Hidden from view, tucked down a cobbled back street which barely saw the light of day, the attitude of the Victorian city planners was 'well, if needs must'.

Not that the Kenilworth was ever a drinking den. 'The Kenilworth's opulent interior makes it one of the most evocative late Victorian pubs,' wrote Rudolph Kenna and Anthony Mooney in their book *People's Palaces*. 'Behind the pillared island bar counter there is a display stand of pronounced panache, exuberantly carved, mirrored and adorned with palm fronds.' The walls are lined with creamy, pale green tiles – the sort found in a Victorian urinal, though distinctly more fragrant, and above is a lofty Jacobean ceiling. With its main box-shaped single room the Kenilworth may not be the cosiest pub in the world, but it is a real authentic jewel of its kind.

Originally the pub had a long back bar and the ceiling would have been considerably lower. In 1900 Peter Fisher commissioned Thomas Marwick to extend the pub and raise the ceiling. If you look up you can see a second tier of small windows in stained glass where there was once an upstairs flat. Marwick, whose architectural firm also designed churches along with country houses and industrial works, also put in the island bar. Perhaps not surprisingly its main feature looks like a small, ornately carved pulpit. Either way it is not exactly practical for a modern bar according to the current landlord. Not that he can change a thing, of course – the whole building and bar are now listed.

MILNE'S BAR
35 HANOVER STREET EH2 2PJ

Milne's, long known as 'The Poets' Pub', has two entrances; one at street level on Rose Street, the other through the basement on Hanover Street. If there is a Pantheon to modern Scottish literature, it is perhaps here Although now much refurbished and themed, it was here during the 1950s and early 1960s that a group of poets met, talked, drank, smoked and read their works to each other.

It was some group and had as its quasi-godfather – Christopher Murray Grieve who is better known under his published name – Hugh MacDiarmid. Others included Norman MacCaig, Sorley Maclean, Sidney Godsir Smith, Robert Garioch, and the younger poet Alan Bold. Collectively, they represent the best of 20th century Scottish poetry. They also incidentally contributed more than their fair share to the country's brewing and whisky industry. Before his death in 1998, Bold wrote of Milne's' gatherings: 'MacDiarmid alternating between affability and intensity, MacCaig delivering swift, sarcastic verbal thrusts, Smith, with a monocle in his eye and a glass in his hand and sometimes and inhaler to ward off attacks of asthma. All three poets were incessant smokers as well as heavy drinkers, so their presence was surrounded by a tobacco cloud of unknowing.'

Were they alive today, they would have to stand in the street to smoke under the new non-smoking regime. Today Milne's is one of a range of pubs along the Rose Street area, and offers food and respite from the exertions of shopping on Princes Street. The downstairs bar is quieter and more comfortable. But for watching street life on Rose Street through the windows, stay upstairs.

Norman MacCaig, one of the circle of writers who met here, later wrote a poem entitled 'Rose Street – Milne's Bar' which included the lines:

**Cigarette smoke floated
In an Eastern way
A yard above the slopped tables
(Norman MacCaig, *Collected Poems*)**

Because of Hugh MacDiarmid's strong political affiliations, Milne's became known as the 'Little Kremlin'. Many other writers would join the gatherings, including such luminaries as Dylan Thomas, Stevie Smith and W.H. Auden. But today, little remains of the atmosphere of those heady literary days, but with the photos of the writers on the walls and a pint in front of you, while waiting for a meal, you can think back to those evenings here that have produced some of Scotland's best modern poetry.

THE ABBOTSFORD
3 ROSE STREET EH2 2PR

The Abbotsford is a Rose Street institution. Its history is intimately bound with its neighbour across the street – Jenners. The 'Grande Dame of Princes Street', has always been a spiritual home for Morningside ladies in search of retail therapy.

In homage to their loyalty as shoppers, female figures were carved into the columns when the store was rebuilt after a bad fire in 1892. It was reported that firemen fought the blaze from the roof of the Abbotsford Arms, which had opened five years earlier.

In 1902, to make room for an expanding Jenners, the pub was transferred to its present site on the other side of the street. It occupies the ground floor of a Scots Baronial building in red sandstone designed by the prolific pub architect – P.L. Henderson. Built on a grand scale and remarkably well-preserved, the Abbotsford is undoubtedly his greatest surviving pub.

In the middle, stands an imposing beautifully carved island bar in Spanish mahogany – the same wood used for the fittings and panelling. Together with the ornate ceiling it feels Jacobean, sombre and elegant. The year after it opened, the pub was praised for its colour scheme with the upper walls painted green as they still are. Lining the walls are bench seats which fill up at lunchtime as they have for years – this being one of the first Edinburgh pubs to serve food.

Until recently the Abbotsford was run by the Grant family who had been here since 1940.

The original Mrs Grant was part of a fearsome trio of Edinburgh publicans who included Betty Moss of the Old Chain Pier and Miss Scott of Scott's Bar at the far end of Rose Street. If anyone misbehaved or aroused the disapproval of Miss Scott, she would bring her walking stick down on the bar with a deafening crack. They would not be served another drink that night.

Women were allowed into the Abbotsford in the fifties and sixties, though not many ventured this far at least not respectable ones given Rose Street's reputation at the time. With its brothels and massage parlours it was the New Town's street of shame – a riotous red-light district packed with forty pubs in the space of a few hundred yards. To keep the peace, the street had its own policeman who was constantly helping publicans evict unwanted customers. The Friday night drunks were taken off to the police station on the Royal Mile and charged by the bailie in the morning.

By day Rose Street was more sober, but no less busy – there being just one licensed tea shop on Princes Street and nothing but banks and offices on George Street. The Abbotsford also attracted literary types like Sorley McLean, Hugh MacDiarmid and Alan Bold. It was, at least at lunchtime, just as much a poet's pub as Milne's Bar. Among today's writers, Iain Banks pops in from time to time.

THE CAFE ROYAL
19 WEST REGISTER STREET EH2 2AA

In *Let it Bleed*, Ian Rankin's Inspector Rebus drops into the Café Royal: 'It was eleven-fifteen and he was the second customer of the day. He liked the place when it was empty. It was one of the few bars he knew which had less atmosphere the busier it got...' Similarly, In Iain Banks's *Complicity*, Cameron Calley comments on the optical illusion created by the myriad of mirrors: 'I can see those bottles on the gallery ahead of me and I can see their reflections behind them, but I can't see me! I can't see my own reflection!'

The Café Royal is a monument to late Victorian prosperity and self-confidence. It was impressive then, and even more so now, given how few such bars have survived. Today, of course, every inch of its marble-topped counters, hand-painted tiles and wooden panelling is listed. Yet as recently as 1969, the whole building faced demolition had the Council and the Café's previous owners, had their way. Without a public petition condemning the plan, it would have been buried beneath the car park of Woolworth's next door – a fate which even the most ardent modernist would not have wished for. While for lovers of baroque, *fin de siécle* décor, it would have been an act of criminal folly.

The first Café Royal stood across the street in 1826. It was replaced in 1863 by the new Café Royal Hotel on the present site, and was soon advertising bed & breakfast, and 'dinner off the joint', both for 1s 6d. Subsequent alterations in the decade up to 1900 transformed

it into among the most sumptuous bar restaurants in Britain, as each new owner sought to outdo his predecessor. None more than Charles Clark who bought the place in 1898. Clark abandoned the accommodation side of the business and leased out the upper floors to what was ironically a temperance hotel. The focus became food and drink, particularly oysters, which were served 'scalloped, stewed, curried or grilled' at a shilling (5p) per dozen. But for the prices (oysters now start at £7.25 per half dozen), very little has changed since the early 1900s. Still split in two, the Circle Bar has its original semi-circular leather booths by the window and an octagonal island bar in the middle. This is surrounded by brass lamps the shades of which resemble giant ice creams lit from within. The back wall is entirely tiled with a series of life-size murals of famous inventors including Caxton, Watt and Faraday.

The Oyster Bar is separated behind a finely carved walnut screen. Add in the white table-cloths and gleaming glassware, and the effect is even more glitzy. The tiled murals give way to an entire row of stained glass windows behind the bar. The theme is sport and somehow very English apart from the kilted deer stalker. The cricketer looks almost comically pukka as he plays the ball with a straight bat. What one earth would he have made of Cameron Calley – the free-wheeling, substance-abusing, Gonzo hack?

GUILDFORD ARMS
1 WEST REGISTER STREET EH2 2AA

As you might guess from its rotating front door flanked by granite columns, the Guildford Arms was originally a hotel. Before being converted into a bar, it enjoyed a brief moment of fame through one of its barmaids. Miss Lizzie Veitch was a prototype Page 3 girl having won first prize in a beauty contest run by a London paper. The hotel was bought in the mid-1890s by James Dodds, who promptly hired the pub architect Robert Macfarlane Cameron to build him a sumptuous new bar.

Cameron stripped out the hotel's ground floor ceiling to create a lofty space for an oval island bar and a couple of side rooms. Upstairs he installed a mezzanine floor that could seat 100 for 'smoking concerts' – Edinburgh's rather stiff response to London's more raucous music-hall concerts. With its dark mahogany and polished brass all gleaming under gas lamps, it was a magnificent Victorian boozer – a so-called 'people's palace'.

It was built during a golden age of pub design, ironically at a time when the temperance movement was running high. Many city pubs were evil-smelling dives which suited some of the more militant anti-alcohol crusaders whose occasional battle-cry was 'we must make drink stink'. Presumably this was to shame people into sobriety.

A more enlightened approach was to trust people's better nature – that by letting them drink in opulent surroundings their behaviour would be suitably civilised. And just in case it wasn't, the publican was well placed to spot any trouble from his island bar and could wade in quickly before things got out of hand. The authorities took their role as the citizens' nanny very seriously and were inherently suspicious of unsupervised gatherings. If grown-ups were left alone with access to alcohol, who knew what mischief they might get up to!

Though the island bar disappeared decades ago and the mezzanine level has long been a dining area, the Guildford Arms has remained true to its roots. The tall arched windows with the pub's name etched on frosted glass are unchanged, as are the velvet curtains and curved leather banquettes. So too, is the ornate Jacobean-style ceiling with its thick gloss paint which some may find too much. Not that Victorian design was ever exactly minimalist.

The upstairs overlooks the bar from a balcony and features a new bistro with stripped wood floor and funky seats in keeping with the char-grilled menu. From on high you can peer down on the pomp and swirling plasterwork below. It certainly feels like 'the real thing' unlike those ersatz Victorian theme bars tried out by some of the big pub chains.

The Guildford has been family-owned and run since 1896 – and it shows. The family firm, DM Stewart, now boasts six pubs in its small empire having recently acquired the Abbotsford on Rose Street. Independence means being free to choose one's own beer and Deuchars has featured from the start. It sells particularly well here, especially whenever there's a rugby international. On one occasion the entire Scotland squad piled in to celebrate winning the Calcutta Cup over England. The evening grew boisterous, the Deuchars flowed and at some point the cup got damaged. Though, as was later proved, it didn't happen here.

THE DOME & STANDING ORDER
14 GEORGE STREET EH2 2PF
62/66 GEORGE STREET EH2 2LR

For years the main arteries of the New Town were kept free of bars. Wherever possible these were tucked discreetly out of sight within the shady confines of Rose Street. Beyond this oasis, licensed premises were few and far between. For years there was just one licensed tea shop on Princes Street and nothing on George Street.

Seeing George Street today with its flagship stores, restaurants and wine bars, it is hard to imagine it as a sober-suited boulevard full of financiers, insurance agents and solicitors. Anyone wanting a drink at lunch-time or after work had to venture elsewhere. This usually meant Rose Street, though in the street's raucous heyday in the sixties, its bars were not for the faint-hearted.

Above all George Street was where the banks had their headquarters, which stood in lofty splendour, set back from the pavement often behind towering Palladian pillars. None was grander than the head office of the Commercial Bank of Scotland, now the Dome. The site was originally the Physicians Hall, built in 1775 by James Craig, the architect who famously designed the New Town eight years earlier. He went over-budget as architects are prone to do, and presented the College of Physicians with a bill of £4,800, almost double the estimate.

The College moved in, but mounting debts forced them to find someone to purchase the building. They eventually sold out to the Commercial Bank for £20,000 in 1843. The building was then flattened and replaced with a triumphant Graeco-Roman temple copying Playfair's original design for the Surgeons'

Hall. You entered via an imposing hallway with staircases on either side into a vast banking hall with clusters of columns arranged in the shape of a Greek cross.

Then as now the crowning glory is the large decorative cupola in the ceiling. The Dome bar and restaurant was created in the mid-90s when the bank, by then part of the Royal Bank of Scotland, moved out. Most of the original features including the acres of polished marble and granite have been kept.

By coincidence the other great George Street bank – the Union Bank, also opened in 1843 with an imposing Neo-Classical building a few blocks west. It too swapped bank-notes for booze in the mid-nineties to become The Standing Order with a bar the size of a ballroom beneath a ceiling so elaborate it was possibly designed by a pastry chef. Also original are the beautifully etched windows at the back and a massive walk-in safe in an adjoining snug bar. Standing on a plinth beside the bar, is a balding waxwork figure in a grey suit – supposedly an old-style bank manager, though with his ugly snarl and opened brief case full of cash, he looks more like a bank robber from a fifties B movie. Perhaps he's just blown the safe next-door.

The conversion of such buildings marked the end of an era, with George Street no longer Edinburgh's answer to Wall Street. This trend of banks turning into pubs has been replicated in every big city. For Peter Haydon, author of *Beer & Britannia*, the fact it has never happened the other way round is proof that pubs are the more resilient of the two.

THE OXFORD BAR
8 YOUNG STREET EH2 4JB

Visitors to this renowned establishment often have to literally squeeze themselves into the tiny front bar to order a drink but there is a further and cosier back room up a small flight of steps. The Ox, as it is generally known, is a place of pilgrimage for fans of Edinburgh author Ian Rankin's internationally acclaimed Inspector Rebus books. The grumpy fictional Detective Inspector counts this as his favourite pub, if not as his second home. Deuchars is the policeman's preferred brand, with a quality Highland Park 12-year-old single malt whisky as a chaser, and perhaps a Scotch egg as his evening meal.

The creator of the best-selling Inspector Rebus series of novels has also been known to have enjoyed the odd pint or two here as well; amongst the many other writers, journalists and artists who frequent the Ox is Scottish author Iain Banks. The pub is a place for writer-spotting during the Edinburgh International Book Festival in August, which takes place nearby in Charlotte Square Gardens at the end of Young Street. But you are as likely to meet eminent Edinburgh lawyers, amateur football pundits, Irish book reviewers, off-duty policemen or jaded tour guides in this eclectic environment. Or perhaps a group of excited German crime-reading fans hoping to meet Rebus (or Rankin).

A former and legendary owner of the Ox was renowned for his rudeness and could ban

guests to the pub on the grounds of either being female or for having an English accent. One visitor who asked for a gin and tonic was ejected on the grounds of the pub 'not being a cocktail bar'. Gladly, these days are now over, and the pub is a friendly and welcoming howff, but one that has retained its simple qualities in an age when many other pubs in the area have been updated and refurbished.

The Ox has no frills: this is not the place for loud music or fine cuisine. Good soup and rolls are on hand at lunch-times though, and you are almost certain to fall into conversation with one of the many interesting regular customers, many of whom feature (under different guises) in Ian Rankin's books. Indeed, a recent (now retired) owner of the pub is John Gates, who emerges under his own name in the Rebus books as a professor of forensics at Edinburgh University's Medical School, performing autopsies rather than pulling pints. Who knows, if you pop into The Oxford Bar you may meet the Inspector himself – or his creator.

This is also the only pub in the world (at time of writing) that you can sample the unique Highland Park Rebus 20 single malt scotch whisky – created in 2007 to celebrate 20 years of Ian Rankin's Edinburgh detective. This is only at the discretion of Harry the barman and only in return for a donation to charity!

KAY'S BAR
39 JAMAICA STREET EH3 6HF

Given the price of stamps in the early sixties – at least threepence! – firms in Edinburgh employed delivery boys to save money. One such was David Mackenzie whose errands occasionally took him to a tiny wholesaler-cum-licensed grocer on Jamaica Street in the New Town. With its cracked windows and dull, concrete cladding, John Kay & Sons reflected its environment – a rundown backstreet of near derelict tenements. This was in contrast to the surrounding streets with their posh, Georgian terraces. It was said that whenever a Jamaica Street resident was in trouble with the law, which was not uncommon, he could peer into the kitchens and bedrooms across the road and spy on the judge who would try him in the morning. As David recalls, 'Kay's was full of sacks of cereals and loose biscuits.' In the ceiling there was a ring of brass nipples fed by various casks above. People would come to fill their empty bottles with wine, sherry and especially the whisky that Kay's had blended for over a century. The store also supplied the firm's main shop on George Street.

Fast forward to 1976 and this became Kay's Bar – a rival in style and clientele to the Tilted Wig (now the Cumberland Bar). While the property boom has since filled the neighbourhood with sober-suited mortgage payers, back then it was full of well-heeled students whose rent was paid half by the council and half by mummy and daddy. A decade later Kay's Bar was taken on by David Mackenzie who had been running a pub on Broughton Street after a former life selling women's outerwear.

The previous owner of Kay's Bar, had removed the building's ugly cladding to reveal a charming, stone cottage built in 1814, when Jamaica Street was the home of workers and servants servicing the grand houses nearby. He also repainted the interior and ceiling a deep red – the same colour as today. The bar takes up one side and faces two rows of numbered whisky casks where the original Kay's Blend was created. Beneath the ceiling, runs a wooden frieze with the words 'The Glenlivet and Islay Spirit Cellar. Gin, Cognac, Brandy & Claret'.

The décor includes a crimson velvet banquette and small, round tables painted gold. In all, the effect resembles a Victorian theatre, albeit on a miniature scale. Kay's is barely 20 feet long, though there is a small back bar like a library. Whenever a major sporting event is on the telly, the bar can be packed almost literally to the rafters.

Completing the scene is the manager, Fraser, who sports the most magnificent waxed moustache this side of Agatha Christie's *Poirot*. His presence merely confirms Kay's status as a true one-off among the city's bars. It has an incredible club atmosphere particularly in winter when the coal fire is lit, and serves the finest booze. There is good range of cask ales, naturally including Deuchars, and over fifty single malt whiskies.

THE CUMBERLAND
1 – 3 CUMBERLAND STREET EH3 6RT

Apart from Rose Street, which the City Fathers treated as a kind of 'tolerance zone', licensed premises had always been thin on the ground in the New Town. It was as if bars were like betting shops and would deface the classical lines and uniformity of those wide avenues and graceful crescents. Somehow the Cumberland Bar must have slipped through the net. Its only competition apart from Clarks Bar – a fine local and still going strong on Dundas Street, were hotel bars like the Drummond, and later the Claret Jug, beneath the Howard Hotel on Great King Street.

The Cumberland was an old spit 'n' sawdust pub in need of repair when Paddy Crossan took it over in 1970. At the time it would have been full of just men, some of them local and most of them on the silvery side of life. They came for their beer and nips and, perhaps, very occasionally, the odd pie.

This all changed dramatically under the new management. Out went the old floorboards and in came black and white square tiles. Off went the nicotine-stained paint on the ceiling, to be replaced by some American floral wall-paper in pale green and orange that cost £400 a roll – a fortune in those days. Out went the old boozers with their beers and pies and in came bow-tied waiters serving restaurant food, which in turn began to attract women for the first time. And in pride of place behind the bar, a bust of an unknown lawyer was installed. The bust, later known as 'Archie', was a nod to the pub's new name – the Tilted Wig.

The Wig had become a real New Town institution by the time Paddy Crossan sold out to Ian White in 1992, who promptly renamed it the Cumberland Bar. As with the Bow Bar which he also renovated, White had a very clear vision of what he wanted. The chequered tiles were stripped out, the wallpaper carefully steamed off and the whole place panelled in dark wood – much of it coming from disused churches.

With its low ceiling, decorative columns and assortment of snug bars this is how the Cumberland looks today. It remains a popular traditional pub serving good beer and with no blaring TV or jangling jukebox. In summer, its beer garden fills up until an early curfew forces everyone back inside to appease some of the pub's neighbours. For Italians or Spaniards visiting on a balmy evening, this must be particularly hard to understand.

To live in or around Cumberland Street you have to be pretty wealthy these days. Apparently there is a drawer under the bar full of forgotten cheque cards from some of the most exclusive private banks. Among those who have been spotted here having a drink are the comedian Rory Bremner and Prince William, who popped in for a pint of cider despite the owner's self-confessed republican sympathies. The writer Sandy McCall Smith has also been in, presumably, since the Cumberland features in his book *44 Scotland Street*. The street is just round the corner, though the address itself does not exist.

THE BARONY
81 – 85 BROUGHTON STREET EH1 2RJ

Broughton Street flows steeply downhill from Picardy Place at the top of Leith Walk. Just a couple of hundred yards long, this bohemian, self-contained street is packed full of interesting shops, restaurants and cafés. It has an excellent fishmonger in Something Fishy and Crombie's – arguably the best butcher in town. Add in a fruit and veg shop, a newsagent, a few quirky boutiques and some great places to drink and you could almost live here all year round without ever having to stray beyond. It claims to be home to Edinburgh's gay village – though do not expect Sydney or San Francisco, and it boasts no less than six hairdressers!

The Barony Bar is half-way down on the right-hand side. It was named after the ancient barony of Broughton in the parish of St Cuthbert's, which was once a notorious haunt for witches in the dim distant past. They apparently had their own 'witch's howff' or tavern in one of the thatched cottages that stood in what is now Barony Street directly opposite the pub. Meanwhile, those who worshipped the devil or practised witchcraft and other 'Black Arts' were locked in the dungeons of Broughton Street's burgh tollbooth pending execution.

The tollbooth was demolished in 1829, the year before the five-storey townhouse that became home to the Barony Bar was built. At first it was home to an upholsterer and a baker – the one thing Broughton Street now lacks. Then came surgeons, gilders, marble cutters and stationers, until finally the ground floor was turned into a bar in 1898. It was designed by John Forrester, a notable pub architect who gave the Barony its fine, teak frontage with an ornate balcony above.

There is an engagingly relaxed and timeless feel about the Barony with its wonky bar stools and wooden floor and where the TV only comes on for rugby. Large windows at either end fill the place with light during the day. The dark painted ceiling is relatively low and there is a proper log fire in winter, which provides a homely, rustic feel in the heart of Edinburgh. The bar itself – a hefty piece of oak, takes up most of one wall with an extended gantry behind, the nooks and crannies of which are stuffed with single malts and an impressive range of wines by the glass.

It fills up in the evenings and there is live rock music on Sunday nights. About half the punters are locals, though none more than Callum Buchanan whose Metz gallery is literally next door. He calls the Barony 'his office' and has thought of putting in a connecting door from the Metz 'or at least a pipe to let the Deuchars in.' Private view parties tend to end up here as with other galleries in the neighbourhood. As for literary types – well they probably do drink here incognito though the only writer anyone can remember spotting is Irvine Welsh and that was in the Phoenix Bar opposite. The Phoenix is a bit younger, a bit louder and probably has a bit more of an edge.

CASK & BARREL
115 BROUGHTON STREET EH1 3RZ

At the bottom end of Broughton Street, away from the hairdressers and cafés at the top by Piccardie Place, is a big, no nonsense real man's pub in the shape of the Cask & Barrel. It opened in the early nineties and felt like a pub from day one. According to Mitch, the manager, people sometimes come in and think it's the oldest pub in Edinburgh. This sounds a little hard to believe, but it does certainly look a solid, almost timeless, addition to the street.

There had been a bar on the site for years. During the Second World War, it was called the Territorial, though it was half the size – the bigger part being a branch of the Royal Bank of Scotland. It then became the Clearmont Bar and finally the Corner Store which was split into a public and lounge bar with a pool table and darts through the back. By all accounts it was pretty run down when bought by a Mr Macari in 1991.

Macari was a bookmaker whose job often took him to England. He had seen a lot of pubs and wanted to use the best bits from each to create one of his own. With this in mind, he installed a huge horseshoe bar in pale wood with a brass footrest and no stools so that people would stand around and blether. The walls were hung with the mirrors and pictures he had collected on his trips down south. The greatest change

was to demolish the dividing wall between the two bars to create one large space, leaving a massive beam to support several storeys above.

Previously Mitch had been working in the Oyster Bar in Leith, one of the very few real ale bars in town, when Macari poached him for his new venture. For a while he had been coming to the Oyster Bar for its beer which he decided was just what he wanted for the Cask & Barrel. To this day, there's an empty barrel in the middle of the pub, almost always with men clustered round it, while there are barrels etched onto the stained glass that forms the lower part of the windows.

From the outside these windows curve round into London Street to make the most of the pub's corner location. At first the stained glass went quite higher, until it was noticed that women were jumping up to see whether it was a safe place for a drink. Now these have been lowered, more daylight floods in and anyone can take a look. As a result the regulars have become much more mixed. The common theme, whether young or old, male or female, is a liking for good beer. And here the Cask & Barrel, which has served Deuchars from the word go, won't disappoint.

THE BAILIE
2 ST STEPHEN'S STREET EH3 5AL

The Bailie is the start of the St Stephen's Street shuffle – a fifty yard pub crawl that progresses to the Watershed and ends, for those still standing, at the Antiquary. The 'shuffle' can happen any night, but especially after a show by one of the artists from WASPS – a collective of sixty studios, round the corner in Hamilton Place.

As an arty enclave, Stockbridge is not quite the bohemian village it once was. Rising rents and property prices have rather taken the edge off the area, though it feels noticeably more laid-back than the New Town proper. St Stephen's Street still has its boutiques, antique shops and retro second-hand stores a few of which Nico of the Velvet Underground might have known when supposedly living here in the seventies. Across the street there is a pretty stone arch to what was Stockbridge Market and further down the site of Cinderellas Rockerfellers which, in its long life, had been a skating rink, music hall, riding academy, theatre and cinema until it burned down in 1993.

The Bailie is a large, bustling basement pub on the corner with North West Circus Place. The entrance is down a set of steps beneath a wrought iron arch, crowned with a curious, oriental lantern. Dark and spacious, despite the low ceiling, the Bailie has a real subterranean feel. When it is bright and sunny outside, you have to blink to adjust to the black panelled walls, deep red carpet and the maroon, button-back sofas that line the walls.

In the middle there is a big, vaguely triangular island bar. The staff, all dressed in black, are kept busy pulling pints or filling glasses with spirits from the bottles of Scotch, vodka and gin that hang from a central column. Since the smoking ban, food has become much more important especially at lunch-time. Though, be warned, given the absence of daylight and a pile of free newspapers to wade through, lunch can stretch well into the afternoon before you realise. Particularly in the winter beside a real coal fire.

Stockbridge is a delightful part of Edinburgh in which to stroll around and browse. Best of all, when the weather is warm and bright, this is the place to go down onto the Water of Leith and wander half a mile upstream. You can enjoy this delightful, leafy gorge – undoubtedly one of the city's best-kept secrets, before re-emerging by the Gallery of Modern Art to take in an exhibition or simply sit outside the café.

THE ORCHARD
1 HOWARD PLACE EH3 5JZ

Formerly the Northern Bar, the Orchard in Canonmills can be found by the Water of Leith and the Botanic Garden. It is also just a few doors down from 8 Howard Place where Robert Louis Stevenson was born in 1850. The house was damp and none too healthy with all the sewage and effluent that the local mills and tanneries pumped into the river, and before long, his family had decamped to Heriot Row in the heart of the New Town. Yet Stevenson recalled the area of his birth with fondness. In his *Edinburgh: Picturesque Notes*, he wrote that none of his childhood memories compared:

'With the discoverer's joy, and the sense of old Time and his slow changes on the face of this earth, with which I explored such corners as Canonmills or Water Lane, or the nugget of cottages at Broughton Market. They were more rural than the open country, and gave a greater impression of antiquity than the oldest land upon the High Street.'

Under its previous name, it had existed since at least the 1930s, though it is unclear whether there was an earlier bar on the site. Originally it was half the size and shared with a couple of shops – a joiners and a French polishers. It had an island bar, of which only the gantry survived, and must have been packed most lunch-times and evenings. With a printing works, and the offices of banks, insurance firms and the *Scottish Daily Mail* close by, there was a

captive audience during the week and few local bars to compete with. The then Northern Bar bought out the shops and expanded to fill its current space. On the night the *Daily Mail* moved out in 1972, the bar took £750 – a staggering amount in the those days. With beer costing 25p a pint, the local streets must have been awash with drunken hacks on closing time.

Things are a little quieter now with fewer workers coming here since the closure of the Standard Life offices in 1990. But the Orchard remains popular with locals, none more loyal than a certain Sandy McGill who ran the neighbourhood gas works. He became so much part of the furniture he had a hook by the bar to hang his walking stick on, and, when he died, his seat which was taken up by his son who came here almost as often.

This spacious, corner pub is flooded with light when the sun shines, through large, plate-glass windows on two sides. To enhance the effect and to let those sitting here watch the world go by, the split-level wooden floor is raised by the windows. At the far end, there is a area with a flagstone floor where a blue grass session band play every month beneath a sound-proofed ceiling. As for modern literary connections, the Orchard featured briefly in *Gallery Whispers* – one of the Inspector Skinner novels by Quentin Jardine (when it was still the Northern Bar).

THE OLD TOWN & SOUTH SIDE

BENN

USHER & Co
OVG
SPECIAL LIQUEUR

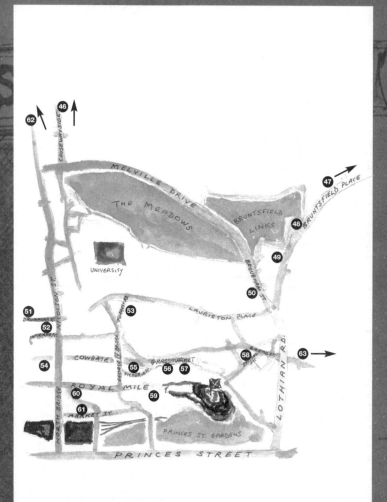

LESLIES BAR
45 RATCLIFFE TERRACE EH9 1SU

D.H. & J. McCallum was a firm of whisky blenders – one of many in late 19th century Scotland hoping to ride the wave as Scotch became a global force. A few like Arthur Bell, Matthew Gloag (as in Famous Grouse) and the Walker brothers of Kilmarnock hit the big-time. Most did not.

In 1894, a McCallum relation – Ann McCallum Middlemas, inherited a property in south Edinburgh on Causewayside. The following year her husband hired the architect P. L. Henderson to replace it with a four storey tenement with a bar and shop. Henderson was a prolific Edinburgh pub designer whose work included the Abbotsford, Deacon Brodie's and the Central Bar in Leith.

The McCallums' nephew, Duncan Stewart, took over the whisky business and later the pub, no doubt hoping the shop would be a great outlet for the McCallum blend. Sadly it was insufficient and the firm was sold to Bell's in 1910, though the name lived on for years. The pub was still selling McCallum's Perfection until the late 1980's.

Leslies, as the pub has been called since John Leslie became the second licensee in 1902, is a classic piece of Victoriana. It soon expanded by swallowing the adjoining shop to allow extra seating in the public bar. The walls were panelled in the fifties in old wood from a neighbouring house that was being renovated, and the ceiling scrubbed clean of pipe-smoke. Otherwise, it's remarkably unchanged – a testament to being family-owned for over a century.

The bar is over 30 feet long and effectively splits the pub in two. Built of solid mahogany, it must weigh a ton. The carved gantry in the middle features stained glass art deco motifs and an original Bryson clock. Having once held casks of whisky, it is now stuffed with bottles of spirits including over sixty single malts.

In 1931 a young man called Alec Smith began working at Leslies. Despite knocking the 'L' off the name when asked to clean the outside, he was allowed to stay. Apart from the war and a period spent living in Australia, Alec worked here until he retired aged 83 in 1998. When he started, the only draught beer was Mackays Original at sixpence a pint. There was a wider range of bottled beers and four whiskies, three of them from D.H. & J. McCallum. For seven pence a nip you could have Leslies Special, or for eight-pence, a drop of Perfection.

With its builders' yards and printing works, Causewayside was then full of light industry, while some of the neighbouring streets of Newington have always been quite genteel. Leslies reflected the social divide. One side was walled off behind a 'snob screen' complete with hatches and curtains that were drawn to keep out prying eyes from the public bar. Each hatch had a bell to ring whenever another drink was required. On the other side of the gantry, Leslies was a spit 'n' sawdust pub with a wooden floor for the workers.

The wall came down, not through revolution, but renovation in the sixties and today there's a democratic swirly-whirly carpet covering the whole pub. A wide mix of people drink in Leslies, including a loyal band of regulars. Asked about anyone famous, the manager replied like a good Edinburgh taxi driver. 'Well, we did have Sean Connery in once.' To be fair, the former 007's parents once lived down the road.

THE VOLUNTEER ARMS (CANNY MAN'S)
237 MORNINGSIDE ROAD EH10 4QU

If ever the ceiling of the Volunteer Arms (or Canny Man's as it is known) collapsed, the drinkers in this legendary Morningside pub would be buried by more than just bricks and mortar. Along with falling masonry, they would be hit by a barrage of antique junk including a pram, a mannequin, a canoe and the entire brass section of a local orchestra. The instruments were left behind as payment for an over-extended bar tab. The mannequin was carried here in the arms of a Canadian airman who had joined a giant conga from the nearby Plaza Ballroom during the VE Day celebrations in 1945. 'It was the wildest party Morningside had ever seen', says the Canny Man's owner, James Watson Kerr.

His great-grandfather had been a drayman for Usher's brewery when he bought the pub in 1871. At the time it resembled a small village inn that had been there since the late 18th century when the area was surrounded by fields. It was converted in the 1890s into the purpose-built pub you see today and was originally 'The Volunteers' Rest' – a reference to the Edinburgh Volunteers who practiced rifle shooting on Blackford Hill. It was John Kerr, the second generation, who was apparently known as the 'the canny (or cautious) man'. The name stuck.

Suspending things from the ceiling simply because you have you have run out of shelf space is just one example of what makes this among the most idiosyncratic and strangely loveable pubs in Edinburgh, if not Britain. But whether you love it or not, the Canny Man's is undeniably original – a true one-off. Being family-owned for so long obviously helps.

The accumulated flotsam of 125 years looks random, but it is all here for a reason whether donated willingly or in lieu of cash. Unlike the sham trinkets and books bought by the yard you'll find in a retro pub, most things here have a story to tell. Take the sabre that hangs above the fire. In 1948 it sliced off the thumb of an army officer who was trying to slice open a bottle of Champagne. The practice, known as Sabrage, has since been banned.

The walls of the main bar are painted a lustrous red to offset the gleaming amber bottles of malt whisky stacked to the rafters. Adjoining this is a large second bar called the 'smokeroom' with tables one end covered in crisp linen where you can choose from a vast selection of open sandwiches or Smørrebrød. Beyond the two bars are a series of discrete snug rooms, one of which opens onto a spacious courtyard in summer.

It is said the Canny Man's was quite a dusty old pub with a crusty management-style. If true, it appears to have mellowed and the mix of people and age groups is much wider than you might think. Women were drinking here in the snug long before they were allowed into most Scottish bars. It has also been freshened up in keeping with its real pride in service. The gents alone deserves a medal as the most fragrant and spotless in town. Where else can a man do what he has to do with fresh-cut flowers on one side and the front of *The Times* thoughtfully taped to the wall in front?

THE GOLF TAVERN
WRIGHT'S HOUSE, BARCLAY PLACE EH10 4HR

Just in case you had missed the name of this famous pub writ large in gold letters above the window, you get the idea pretty much the moment you step inside. As the back wall declares in bold script, this is the 'Home of Golf'. Signed photographs of Tiger Woods, Jack Nicklaus and just about every other golfing hero you can think of, line the walls. These carry on up the stairs to the restaurant above. Here, in pride of place in the corner, is the golf bag of Seve Ballesteros, chained to the wall just in case. There is also a framed set of golf balls signed by every US President from Richard Nixon to George W. Bush. The inclusion of 'Dubya', meant the collection had to be hidden from view in 2005 when the G8 Summit descended on Scotland and Bob Geldof marched against poverty.

As a shrine to the ancient game, it feels as though a small piece of St Andrew's has sheared off and landed on the south side of Edinburgh. Yet the theme of the Golf Tavern is certainly legit, this being the oldest surviving clubhouse in the world. The Bruntsfield Links Golfing Society was formed in 1788 and met here until 1890. People have played golf on the Links since at least the 17th century and it is thanks to them that this open stretch of grassland above the Meadows still exists. From the start they were forever defending their rights to play against those who wanted to dig quarry pits, graze cattle or build roads.

One early golfer was the poet Allan Ramsay. In his 'Elegy on Maggy Johnston' dedicated to the woman who ran a celebrated Bruntsfield tavern until her death in 1711, he wrote:

**'Whan we were weary'd at the Gouff
Then Maggy Johnson's was our Houff'**

Ye Olde Golf Tavern, as it became in Victorian times, claims to date from 1456, although it was probably built in the mid-to-late-18th century. Many of the city's leading brewers drank here as members of the Bruntsfield Links Golfing Society including Robert Clark and George Lorimer – the founders of the Caledonian Brewery in 1869. No doubt they formed their business plan to build what is now home to Deuchars over copious flasks of ale at the Tavern.

Whether they would recognise the place now is another matter. The outside looks 'ye olde worlde' enough with its exposed stonework, mullioned windows and sandstone cladding, but the interior is something else. Chunky bar-stools in steel and soft grey leather cluster round a large kidney-shaped bar topped with aluminium while the low ceiling is studded with spotlights. There are plasma screens and the bar staff are all in black with hands-free phones clipped to their ears. Today's Golf Tavern is one of the most contemporary sports bars in Scotland.

BENNETS BAR
LEVEN STREET EH3 9LG

In the dark days of the seventies, dubbed 'the decade taste forgot', Bennets Bar was one of a handful of Edinburgh pubs that managed to survive the rigours of rebranding unscathed. Just as well, as this is a real, authentic gem. Entering Bennets, you leave behind an ugly stretch of the Lothian Road. The outside traffic is blocked out by frosted glass windows decorated with art deco flowers in pale blue, orange and purple. The windows also advertise Andrew Usher's OVG, or 'Old Vatted Glenlivet' – the world's first real brand of Scotch whisky. Created in the mid-19th century, Usher aimed to smooth out inconsistencies in the famous Speyside malt by vatting, or blending different vintages. From here it was a short step to creating blended Scotch – the drink that made the Usher family fortune, part of which was donated to the city to build the Usher Hall.

There has been a pub here on Leven Street since 1839 on the site of an old ironmonger's. At first it was probably the tap bar for the Taylor MacLeod brewery next door, which has long since disappeared and been replaced by the King's Theatre. The present design of the pub was by the architect George Lyle in 1891 when it was known as Marshall's Bar. You can still see the name painted on the side wall nearest the theatre – as 'Marshall's wines & spirits'. Like most pubs at the time, it would have been active as an off-license selling carry-outs through what is now the snug bar by the entrance. It would also have blended and matured its own whisky and there are still

decorative casks on the gantry which would have once held Marshall's own blend. The King's Theatre opened in 1906. In response the pub doubled in size no doubt expecting a roaring trade in pre- and post-theatre drinks. A back bar was added, now called the Saloon Bar Green Room, designed by the same architect George Lyle. He also improved the main part of the pub which remains pretty much as it was today.

Bennets is a cosy, box-shaped pub with a long bar and magnificently carved gantry behind that is topped with a clock. The Edwardian décor could feel gloomy with all its dark, polished wood, but this is offset by a line of arched mirrors facing the bar. Between the mirrors there are tiles painted with classical figures that could almost have walked in from the theatre next door – as assorted spear carriers and extras in some Greek tragedy.

As a place to smoke, drink and learn your lines, countless actors have found Bennets Bar far more conducive than the theatre itself. As a result whole pantomimes have been rehearsed here, though not in costume. With the smoking ban in pubs, it may force the odd rehearsal into the street, which will entertain anyone waiting at the bus-stop. As well as opening night parties at Bennets there is also a tradition of using the snug bar during performances. This tiny space is cosy for two, let alone fifteen members of the orchestra piling in for a dram in the interval!

CLOISTERS
26 BROUGHAM STREET EH3 9JH

The question of what makes a good pub or bar, is of course highly subjective – everyone has their own view. But it does seem that a clear vision on the part of the owners is important. A place that is unsure of its audience and seeks to be all things to all people can end up being not very much to no-one in particular. Some try too hard to entertain with their 24 hour multi-channel TV and non-stop music as though terrified of being quiet for a second. A pub is essentially a very simple idea – just four walls and a supply of drink. What makes the difference are the people who use it, and often all they require is a warm, convivial space in which to gather.

This may go some way to explain why the Cloisters in Tollcross is a such a popular pub. And it is very much a pub rather than a bar. With its large, rustic fireplace and whitewashed walls, the Cloisters would not look out of place in a West Country market town. It has a relaxed, homely and almost well-worn feel which is quite an achievement given its youth. The Cloisters has only existed as a pub since the early nineties. Before that it was a greasy spoon.

Originally it was the 'All Saints Parsonage' the building being physically joined to the Episcopalian St Michael & All Saints next door – 'confessions 10am or by appointment'. Both were clearly built in the same era, giving the old parsonage the same arched windows as the church.

This ecclesiastical theme continues inside the pub with old pews clustered round the fireplace while the bar itself is made out of wood salvaged from a deconsecrated church. The gantry behind, which takes up the whole of the back wall, is carved in a similar style and features blue stained glass. Perhaps it once held hymn books before the demon drink took over. Today its shelves are stuffed with spirits including around 80 single malt whiskies. You can also buy wines by the glass including champagne.

The real focus however, has always been beer – particularly cask ales like Deuchars, as you can tell from the impressive row of pump handles lining the bar. As part of a tiny chain that includes the Bow Bar above the Grassmarket and the Anchor Inn near St Abb's Head, the Cloisters is heavily into real ale. In fact it was the very existence of such pubs in Edinburgh that inspired the team at the Caley Brewery to create Deuchars in the first place.

Regulars are a mix of doctors, lawyers and teachers alongside 2nd and 3rd year students It attracts plenty of female drinkers and sponsors a women's football team on the Meadows. As for people you might have heard of, the pub did get a surprise visit from the actor David Soul, formerly Hutch of 'Starsky & Hutch', when he was performing at the King's Theatre nearby. And the entire English rugby team once squeezed itself in here, though not in 2006 after their bruising defeat at Murrayfield when the Scots won the Calcutta Cup.

THE BRASS MONKEY
14 DRUMMOND STREET EH8 9TU

To walk into a bar and be confronted by a picture of Jack Nicolson from *The Shining* might put you off your lunchtime drink. But here it doesn't. The iconic photo of the Hollywood actor blends into the background in this supremely relaxed student bar. He features alongside posters of Jimi Hendrix and a host of other film and rock stars.

The Brass Monkey was created a few years ago on the site of a no-nonsense working men's boozer called Stewart's. The transformation has been complete, not least in the extremely comfortable back room, which is dressed in retro 'hippy' style with its oriental carpets and couches. It feels a little like a slice of Marrakech in the heart of Edinburgh. All that is missing apart from the heat and dust, is an active hubbly-bubbly – no chance of that in smoke-free Scotland. And as you stretch out and chill just try not to drip your pint over the carpet.

From the front of the bar, you can look out on Drummond Street, which was completed in the early 19th century and has fragments of the old city walls built after the battle of Flodden at one end. Across the street is one of Edinburgh's great literary bars from the past – Rutherford's, which dates back to 1834.

It was a watering hole for both Robert Louis Stevenson and Arthur Conan Doyle when they studied just up the road at Edinburgh University. Other writers who were regulars included J.M. Barrie and Hugh MacDiarmid. What Stevenson would make of Rutherford's now is another question. With its wooden façade topped with a carved balustrade, it somewhat resembles the Barony on Broughton Street, albeit a poor man's Barony with its peeling paint and windows behind rusting wire mesh. The interior looked scruffy and forlorn, though this may change as the pub was unofficially up for sale at the time of writing.

In 1888, Robert Louis Stevenson had the following flashback as he records in a letter to his great friend Charles Baxter: 'All of a sudden I had a vision of – Drummond Street. And when I remembered that I hoped and feared as I pickled about Rutherford's in the rain and the east wind: how I feared I should make a mere shipwreck…how I hoped I should possibly write one little book.' Stevenson's 'little books' turned out to be *Treasure Island, Kidnapped, Catriona* and many more. So why not buy a paperback copy from Blackwell's bookshop round the corner, order up a pint and settle in for a few hours at the Brass Monkey.

THE ROYAL OAK
1 INFIRMARY STREET EH1 1LT

The Royal Oak is at the top of Infirmary Street, off South Bridge, beside Blackwell's bookshop – formerly known as James Thin's. Around the corner on Nicholson Street and opposite the Old College Quad of Edinburgh University with its massive entrance and dome completed by the architect Playfair, is an upstairs Chinese restaurant. This was previously a simple café where a young single mother called Joanna Rowling sat with her cup of coffee and created Harry Potter. The other fictional character known around these parts, is Detective Inspector John Rebus, Ian Rankin's hard-bitten hero, who has sat brooding over his pint in the corner of 'the Oak'. He may have come in from one of his many visits to the Edinburgh City mortuary at the foot of Infirmary Street.

Before it became the Oak, the pub was named the Pivot and was a haunt of loyal Jambos, as in Jam Tarts or Hearts football fans when it was owned by the former Heart's player Alan Anderson. Today the Royal Oak is one of Edinburgh's prime venues for live Scottish folk music in the evenings, whether in the small bar upstairs or in the 'Wee Folk Club' downstairs. It is especially popular during the Edinburgh Fringe in August when the bar stays open until four in the morning.

For the past few years the Royal Oak has been owned and managed by May Mackenzie and her daughter Heather, who have continued the pub's tradition of encouraging both professional and amateur live folk music. Amongst the many recorded Scottish folk musicians who have developed their careers here are Phil Cunningham, Alastair MacDonald, Ewan Forfar, Bobby Nicholson and the group Aberfeldy.

The Wee Folk Club in the bar below has been running at the Royal Oak since the late nineties and can seat around 40. It offers an intimate atmosphere and the chance to hear some of the best contemporary folk music in the country. Informal 'open-mic' sessions take place in the upstairs bar with musicians just finding space in the corner and playing, sometimes accompanied by the bar's venerable upright piano. If you are feeling brave and want to play a tune or two, there are a couple of battered guitars on the shelf above the entrance.

Just opposite the pub is a plaque marking the site of the city's first public hospital built in 1729 – Edinburgh's first Royal Infirmary, and at the foot of the street, lies the former Royal High School which Sir Walter Scott attended in 1779. The boys were instructed in all subjects, including Greek and Latin, and those clever enough, (Walter Scott amongst them) would leave school at twelve to attend the University up the road and graduate at the age of fifteen. Behind High School Yards at the end of Infirmary Street, you can walk into a secluded area (part of the University) and view the plaque that commemorates the first College of Surgeons in Edinburgh built in 1697. Another one is dedicated to Elsie Inglis, Scotland's latterday answer to Florence Nightingale, who served as a nurse in France and Serbia during World War I and died in 1917.

SANDY BELL'S
25 FORREST ROAD EH1 2QH

In 2001, young American journalist Robert Gold spent a year working behind the bar at Sandy Bell's. On returning home to Michigan, he wrote the following for his local paper: 'The determination to land this job, had nothing to do with the ales, stouts and lagers waiting to be served. It was because the pub is the social centre of Scotland. It's the dinner party, card game and counselling session rolled into one.'

Yet this particular pub's real purpose in life was something else. 'As 6 o'clock came round, the familiar musical faces would stroll in, lugging their fiddles, guitars, flutes and drums. Soon the night would be filled with lively tunes from a revolving door of 15 or so musicians.'

Sandy Bell's is the city's original and best known venue for live folk music, whether home-grown or far flung. Names that have played here include Ali Bain, Phil Cunningham, The Dubliners and Barbara Dickson in her early years. Emily Lou Harris and Nils Lofgren have also been spotted here. There is live music every night of the week that builds to an invariably packed house by Friday and Saturday. Not that it takes much to pack this pint-sized Scottish pub, which probably holds the world record for the greatest number of musicians squeezed into the smallest possible space.

With the music came poets, writers, artists and singers who mingled with students from the University nearby. In the midst of all this for much of the last fifty years was the tall, shambling figure of Hamish Henderson whose bust sits above the bar. Henderson was a poet, part-time communist, historian and tireless collector of folk songs who fought alongside Italian partisans during World War II. He died in 2002, having spent much of his life in the pub he called his 'office'.

It was originally the Forrest Hill Bar, a conversion of an earlier grocer's shop in the late-19th century. It became known as Sandy Bell's after the landlady's brother-in-law at some point in the sixties. It was built on the site of an old poorhouse after Forrest Road was created to give access to Greyfriar's Kirk and what is now the oldest graveyard in the city, where 1200 Covenanters were imprisoned in 1679. Later came tales of the so-called 'resurrection men' (later the title of an Inspector Rebus novel) who would steal fresh corpses and then sell them to the University's anatomy department with no questions asked.

Many eminent Scots are buried here including the poet Allan Ramsay and James Craig – architect of the New Town. But all rest in peace, untroubled by the steady stream of tourists who come only to lay flowers and cuddly toys at the headstone of Greyfriars Bobby. The Skye terrier who faithfully visited the grave of his master every day until it died in 1872, was made famous by Eleanor Atkinson's book forty years later and by Disney in the 1949 film. Since when Scotland's answer to Lassie has had his own statue and his own pub – the Greyfriar's Bobby – which also serves Deuchars, and rightly so.

BANNERMAN'S BAR
55 NIDDRY STREET EH1 1LG

'You stared down from the South Bridge, and instead of a stream you see the Cowgate, the dirtiest, narrowest, most densely peopled of Edinburgh streets,' wrote Alexander Smith in 1865. Flowing east from the Grassmarket, the Cowgate is a dark canyon that is fed by even darker closes, where the city's poor lived like troglodytes. From the safety of the bridge, they could be viewed 'scrambling into, or oozing out of, public houses, lodging houses, or missions,' according to Smith's contemporary, Alasdair Alpin MacGregor.

Today's troglodytes in this netherworld of clubs and bars are mostly students plus the odd fictional reporter like Jack Parlabane, a character in Christopher Brookmyre's novel *Quite Ugly One Morning,* who comments on the 'shadowy caverns' that make Bannerman's 'quite the most conducively conspiratorial drinking establishment'.

Bannerman's Bar sits at the foot of the South Bridge, its massively thick walls supporting eight stories of masonry above. The bridge was built from a series of vaults stacked like egg-boxes on top of each-other. These were sold off in lots by the Trustees of the South Bridge on condition that whoever bought them would build a tenement. Over the years the site of Bannerman's has been home to leather merchants, flax-dryers, bakers and workshops until it finally became a bar in 1979.

The bar area has a primeval feel with its blackened stone walls and flagstone floor. There are scuffed leather sofas and a ceiling draped with banners and flags, but little else to soak up the noise coming from the 'Underworld' next-door. Here up to ninety bands a month play, some of them for the first time in public. Would-be rockers are encouraged to send in CDs by a friendly website – 'the worst we'll say is no'.

Music has been central to Bannerman's from the start, and though it has moved on from mainly folk to mainly rock, the range is eclectic and attracts a far wider audience than you might think. People of very different ages come to hear everything from ska to tribute bands playing their respects to the late Jim Morrison. The biggest recent name was the Scottish singer-songwriter K.T. Tunstall.

Whether she knew it, or not,Tunstall was playing on the site of an old oyster bar, one of many the Cowgate was famous for in the late-18th century when men came to dine, drink rum punch and watch the ladies dance. The 'Underworld' was a bricked-up vault until it was knocked through in the early eighties. The guys from Bannerman's found it knee-deep in rubble and oyster shells.

A terrible fire that swept through the Cowgate on the night of 7th December 2002 could have been the end of this 'conducively conspiratorial drinking establishment'. Bannerman's survived thanks to a lack of strong wind and some very brave firemen who contained the blaze to the other side of the bridge.

BOW BAR
80 WEST BOW EH1 2HH

At the east end of the Grassmarket, a pretty, cobbled street rises in a steep curve to join the North Bridge. Victoria Street, or the West Bow as it's partly called, makes a nice contrast to the Royal Mile above. The West Bow delights in its slightly quirky boutiques, delicatessens, restaurants and a great little pub called the Bow Bar. It is a traditional single-roomed tavern with a dark wooden floor and a bar that stretches the length of the pub. Lining the wall opposite there is a row of ancient, padded leather benches. Above these hang various, etched mirrors advertising the beers of forgotten breweries and old cigar brands.

Though it seems as old as the street, the Bow Bar was in fact conceived in the early 1990s by a man called Ian White who specialised in restoring old pubs and then selling them on. Not that this was actually a pub before. It previously struggled on under another name as 'a sort of honky-tonky pub restaurant' to quote the current owner, Bill Strachan. One night it caught fire, and the place was completely gutted. This gave Ian White a blank canvas to create what he wanted using old wood from deconsecrated churches to build the bar, benches from disused railway stations and original mirrors bought at auction.

The Bow Bar has a special place in the history of the Caledonian Brewery, being the first pub to serve Deuchars. The commitment to cask ales has been there from the start though English visitors might wonder why there are small brass taps in place of the usual beer handles you would find in a similar pub down south. Here they employ an old Scottish system that has all but died out, where compressed air is used to gently raise the beer from the cellar. Apparently it is harder than it looks and easy to send beer foaming all over the bar if you get it wrong.

The pub's dedication to real ale has won it a stash of awards from the drink's campaigning body – CAMRA. Apart from beer enthusiasts, regulars include lawyers, judges, off-duty policemen, council workers, local shopkeepers and tourists who have broken free from their tour guides. And, though miles from Murrayfield, it does attract a crowd during rugby matches – one of the few times the TV is switched on.

The Bow Bar is also one of the best whisky bars in town. With around 145 drams on offer there are malts here from distilleries that no longer exist. The rarest available at the time of writing was a 37-year-old John Scott's Highland Park from Orkney which was selling for £13.95 a nip. All the whiskies, together with their age, strength and type of cask are recorded in a book – an idea that came from watching two regulars systematically drink their way through the entire range. They did pace themselves however – two at a time every Saturday morning.

THE LAST DROP
74 GRASSMARKET EH1 2JR

There was nothing like a good hanging to get the Old Town out on the streets. The original site for public executions had been Castle Hill and Mercat Cross, but by the mid-17th century it had moved down to the Grassmarket. The gibbet stood near the city well at the foot of the West Bow, not far from the the Last Drop pub. It was written that 'the human shambles of this place of wailing, witnessed executions of this kind almost daily till the 17th February 1688.' This was the date when the last of over 100 Covenant martyrs, James Renwick, was executed. Earlier the Duke of Rothes had said of one stubborn protester – 'Then let him glorify God in the Grassmarket.'

The gibbet continued to operate, though at a less frenetic pace. It was not used however, for the most famous public hanging, that of Captain Porteous, commander of the City Guard, in 1736. Porteous had overseen the execution of a man for smuggling – considered a victimless crime against the Old Enemy; the English – and had then ordered his men to fire on the crowd when it began to riot. He was arrested and sent for trial, but when it appeared he was about to be pardoned, the mob stormed the city Tollbooth where he was hiding up a chimney, and dragged him down the West Bow to his fate. They broke into Robert Cresser's brush shop en route, left a guinea on the counter for a length of rope, and then strung up the unfortunate Captain from a dyer's pole. The pub's name is obviously a nod to all this, though the actual 'last drop' round here

was in 1785 – this time a state execution rather than a lynching. Today the only blood spilt might be the occasional Friday night punch-up – somehow more likely from the rougher Cowgate end than the Grassmarket itself. On a balmy summer's evening the year-round smokers on the pavement chairs are joined by others to give Edinburgh a dose of Continental street life.

The Last Drop, is a friendly, rough and tumble sort of pub with slap 'n' dash plaster walls in cream, and with areas of exposed stone. There is a bleached wood floor to contrast the dark stained tables and chairs, and comfy banquettes in scuffed, coffee-coloured leather. A few 'ye olde worlde' candles hang from the low ceiling and the overall lighting is yellowy and subdued. This gives the Last Drop a perennial 'late afternoon' feel, until the evening rush kicks in.

'The best chicks hang out at the Drop' declares a large sign with characters from the film *Chicken Run*, while the rafters are plastered with foreign bank notes. Clearly the pub gets plenty of overseas visitors, though they are probably outnumbered by students. Not the sort ever taught by the likes of Miss Jean Brodie however. In her famous novel, Muriel Spark takes this 'Edinburgh spinster of the deepest dye' on a tour of the Grassmarket where she shows her 'gels' another side of city life to the gentility of 1930s Bruntsfield.

THE WHITE HART
521 LAWNMARKET EH1 2PE

The name of this historic pub overlooking the Grassmarket comes from one of the city's earliest legends in which King David I was almost gored to death by a huge white stag while out hunting in 1128. He was saved when a fiery cross appeared between the animal's antlers causing it to vanish. In gratitude, King David founded Holyrood Abbey.

The White Hart is not that old, although parts of the cellar date back to 1516. The building above was constructed in 1740, though the interior of the pub is far more recent. It was a classic 18th century coaching inn that offered a ringside seat whenever there was a public hanging. Though it was not for this that the great bard Robert Burns stayed here for a week in November 1791. Four years earlier Burns had re-established contact with his wife, Jean Armour, to the extent of getting her pregnant for the second time. A few months later however, he fell madly in love with the young Mrs Agnes M'Lehose. Using the pen-names 'Sylvander' and 'Clarinda', letters began to fly back and forth full of yearning and sighing. The stay at the White Hart, was to say goodbye to 'Clarinda' who was due to sail from Leith to seek reconciliation with her estranged husband in Jamaica. The parting inspired the following lines which are now inscribed on the beams of the pub in between the ranks of pewter tankards that hang there:

Ae fond kiss, and then we sever!
Ae fareweel, Alas for ever!
Deep in heart-wrung tears I'll pledge thee,
Warring sighs and groans I'll wage thee.

In September 1803, the poet William Wordsworth and his wife Dorothy, also stayed here at the end of a six week, rain-soaked tour of the Highlands in an open-topped carriage. In 1828, the inn was supposedly one of the haunts favoured by that evil double-act Burke and Hare. They would entice their victims back to their lodgings nearby where they could be murdered in peace and then sold to Dr Knox for his anatomy classes. In the words of the popular rhyme – 'Burke's the butcher, Hare's the thief. Knox the boy who buys the beef.'

Then on the night of 16th April 1916, the White Hart received a direct hit from a Zeppelin that had drifted in over Leith and St Andrew's Square during Edinburgh's only air raid of World War I. The Inn survived and remains popular with students, tourists and those interested in the paranormal. A few years ago, the then manager invited the city's 'Ghost Club Council' to spend the night here. Over the years there had been sightings of shadowy figures behind the bar, and the sound of creaking barrels and of doors slamming. A report of their vigil, records loud, unexplained banging noises, sudden surges in electromagnetic current and the presence of a young woman and a man in a tricorn hat. Despite this, the report concluded it was 'a very enjoyable night in a cosy pub.'

THE BLUE BLAZER
3 SPITTAL STREET EH3 9DX

For some reason theatres and red light districts often go hand in hand as they do in London's West End. The same is true of Edinburgh where the tangle of streets behind the Usher Hall and the Lyceum Theatre is affectionately known as the 'pubic triangle'. Bang in the middle, stands a magnificent late Victorian pub called the Blue Blazer on the corner of Bread Street and Spittal Street. 'With a bookie's on one side, a chippie on the other, and a sex shop two doors down, what more could you want?' asks the landlord, tongue firmly in cheek.

The Blazer is part of what was the Clan Alpine Building, built in 1864. Originally there was a pair of shops here that changed hands until bought by James Sommerville, a wine and spirits merchant from Leith in 1889 for £1000. By the turn of the century it had become Flanagan's Bar, named after the first tenant.

It only became the Blue Blazer in the mid-seventies. The name was proudly painted above the door in gold, and a large circular mosaic featuring a blue blazer was laid on the parquet floor. Otherwise it remains largely untouched with its black, embossed wallpaper, high ceiling and ornate cornicing. There is a fine, carved gantry and, above, a series of sawn-off barrels from the Harviestoun Brewery now part of the Caley empire. The walls are decorated with old whisky adverts. These include Meg Dod's 'Special Brew' – Meg, being a fearsome Glasgow dame in a frilly bonnet, and Dewar's whose early ads invariably featured a moustachioed, monocle-wearing pillar of the Establishment.

The Blue Blazer has always been popular with actors who come to read through scripts or wind down after a performance. On one memorable occasion an entire orchestra piled in – a daunting sight for the barman who was on his own that night. More recently the Irish actor, James Nesbitt was outside filming a scene from Christopher Brookmyre's *Quite Ugly One Morning*. By strange coincidence the Blazer's manager then on duty was James Nisbet. So with pints poured and amidst much laughter, Nisbet and Nesbitt were photographed together behind the bar.

THE ENSIGN EWART
32 GRASSMARKET EH1 2JU

The Ensign Ewart, at the top of the Lawnmarket, is the closest pub to Edinburgh Castle, which brings in a steady stream of tourists. Those just wanting to use the loo are politely turned away. Those who stay can expect good beer, malt whisky, decent pub food and warmth. Come the evening, things quieten down with a few regulars mingling with those passing through.

Yet what history this pub must have witnessed in over three centuries! Part of the cellar dates back to at least 1590, and there's still a door, scarred with ancient graffiti, that originally opened onto the street. This was raised by twelve feet in the mid-17th century when Edinburgh was struck by the Plague. The bar, known as the 'Hole of the Wall' was suddenly plunged underground. Merchants from the Lawnmarket would gather here for their 'meridian' – a noonday drink signalled by the bells of St Giles. Later the same bells tolled the 'tinkle sweetie' to announce the end of the working day at 8pm and time for some serious drinking

The bar was now part of Milne's Court – a pioneering piece of real estate from the 1690s – whose flats cost as much as £6000 Scots, a fortune for its day. The leading merchants, nobles and even an ambassador lived here. Outside passed armies attacking or defending the Castle, state processions, and those condemned to the scaffold – including Edinburgh's last witch who was strung up in 1702. A century later and the area was starting to decline as the wealthy fled for the space and grandeur of the New Town. For writers like Stevenson and Scott these streets became a rich source of inspiration.

In 1899 St Leonard's brewery bought the bar and renamed it the Eagle – the emblem of the Scots Greys, famous for their cavalry charge at Waterloo. The regimental hero was Charles Ewart, a 45-year old sergeant from Kilmarnock. 'One [of the French] made a thrust at my groin,' he later wrote. 'I parried him off and cut him down through the head. A lancer came at me – I threw the lance off my right side and cut him through the chin and upwards through the teeth'... and so on, until Ewart captured the French standard.

With Scottish regiments regularly stationed at the Castle, the military connection was always strong. It became the Ensign Ewart in 1964, just after Milne's Court had become a Halls of Residence for Edinburgh University. Not that many of the 400 students dared venture into what was now a real 'squaddies pub'. The fights were spectacular and the police seldom far away. By the time the current landlord took over in 1985, the pub had a dire reputation. But banishing the squaddies and bringing in live music, decoration and much softer lighting soon helped restore the Ensign Ewart. Today it remains a cosy refuge in this, the highest, most windswept part of the Old Town.

THE ALBANACH BAR
179 HIGH STREET EH1 1PE

In 2004 Ian Rankin wrote one of his best Inspector Rebus books. The title was taken from a tiny side-street in the heart of the Old Town, where the skeletons of a mother and child were found in a cellar buried in concrete. 'Fleshmarket Close, was a narrow, pedestrian-only lane connecting the High Street to Cockburn Street. The High Street entrance was flanked by a bar and a photographic shop ... [the other] entrance boasted a bookmaker's one side, and a shop opposite selling crystals and 'dream-catchers': old and new Edinburgh, Rebus thought to himself.'

The bookmaker's has since disappeared – another victory for 'new Edinburgh' in Rebus's eyes. In its place stands a boutique selling T-shirts for babies with slogans like 'Daddy's little devil' and 'it's cool to drool'. The shop selling crystals is still there, as is the bar though when *Fleshmarket Close* was written, it was called EH1. Today EH1 is the thoroughly modern, spruced up Albanach Bar – the result of a complete makeover by its new owners in 2005. The old plaster walls have been excavated right back to the original 18th century stone, and the floor covered in stripped pine all the way to the bistrot area at the back. Here a large bow window looks out over Cockburn Street one floor down.

A lot of effort has been lavished on the Albanach, which lifts this bar above others on the Royal Mile with their gloomy fug and beer-soaked carpets. The design mixes the rustic and the contemporary with rough-hewn walls and weathered beams on one hand, and a polished granite bar fronted by chunky wire

cables on the other. The modern art on display attempts to reflect this mix. There are boulders suspended from the ceiling in rope cradles like giant hams, and a length of driftwood beneath a five foot stretch of rusty barbed wire. The work is entitled 'atharrai cidh an tir ach chan atharraich an cridh' – words beyond the ken of a computer's spellcheck.

This inviting, brightly-lit space is in contrast to the sinister dive you might expect being on the corner of a street called Fleshmarket Close whose name suggests Burke and Hare – Edinburgh's notorious 19th century body snatchers. In fact the Fleshmarket was simply the name of the old meat market here. The Close originally led down to a slaughterhouse beside the Nor'Loch, now the site of Princes Street Gardens. According to Lord Cockburn, the loch was 'a fetid and festering marsh, the receptacle for skinned horses, hanged dogs, frogs and worried cats.'

The Nor'Loch was drained in 1787, when that other Edinburgh bogie man – Deacon Brodie, was living his double-life of upright citizen by day and burglar by night. Here there is a direct connection to the Albanach, which stands on the site of James Clarke's Tavern one of Brodie's favourite haunts. Here he drank, chased women, gambled on cockfights and generally lived beyond his means as a craftsman. To escape debt he turned to crime until he was caught and sentenced to death. On 1st October 1788 he swung from the town gibbet, which he had helped to design.

THE DORIC TAVERN
15 MARKET STREET EH1 1DE

The Doric Tavern on Market Street is slap in the middle of Edinburgh, squeezed beside Waverley Station at the foot of The Mound where the New and the Old Town meet. Yet the original building was built in the early 18th century, long before the New Town or the railways were conceived. The property belonged to Robert Mylne, a Jacobite writer of satirical verse, who died in 1747 aged 103, or thereabouts, having outlived all but one of his 12 children. The property passed to his grand-nieces in Aberdeen whose dialect is known as Doric which could explain the Tavern's name.

Market Street was originally on the edge of the city beside the Nor' Loch, now Princes Street Gardens. By the time it was drained and planted with flowers, the loch had become a vast, open sewer full of the Old Town's filth. The Tavern was originally used by a flax dresser and then a brushmaker from 1804 until the railways steamed into town in the mid-19th century. The ground floor then became the Northern Tavern run by a Mr Chicken followed by the Currie family until it was taken over by Usher's brewery in 1898.

Skip forward to the 1960s, and the Doric was acquired by Jimmy McGuffie, a former head porter at the Balmoral Hotel. McGuffie's genius was to create a modern, popular bistro when Edinburgh was woefully short of decent restaurants. A bohemian crowd, including journalists from the nearby *Scotsman,* would jostle for one of three sittings of lunch and dinner upstairs. Ties and jackets were required, though these could be borrowed.

Eventually other restaurants started poaching customers from the Doric whose frilly cuisine began to seem dated. It flirted briefly with being 'Edinburgh's first wine bar', but the idea was ahead of its time. In complete contrast, the downstairs bar would be full of railwaymen, bus drivers and barrow boys from the fruit market opposite. McGuffie died in the early eighties and for a couple of years the Doric was run by the old staff until the hotelier Rayner Voss took over in 1985.

With a personal love of the arts, and various artists for chefs, Voss turned the upstairs into an unofficial gallery. He would tour the Edinburgh College of Art degree shows and offer to display the works he liked for free. Foremost among these were the paintings of Callum Innes. As with restaurants during McGuffie's heyday, there was a dearth of galleries in the city and the Doric played an important role. The arty connection has since waned, though the walls still display works by an artistic sous-chef among others including a limited edition Matisse print. In terms of food, the upstairs bistro remains deservedly popular – a true survivor despite intense competition. Meanwhile the ground floor, now known as 'McGuffie's', has changed dramatically in line with the surrounding area. Just as the old fruit market is now a gallery, so downstairs is no longer a rough, working men's pub. Today, with its good beer and freshly-cooked food from the kitchen above, it attracts a much more mixed crowd than ever before.

SHEEP HEID INN
43 THE CAUSEWAY, DUDDINGSTON EH15 3QA

How often can you have a drink in a bar that boasts its own Victorian bowling alley and dates back to 1360, making the Sheep Heid Inn, (pronounced heed, not head) far and away the oldest licensed premises in town. The Inn being in Duddingston however, this was not officially part of Edinburgh until the 1890s. Even now, this is easily the most self-contained of all the city's villages, shielded by Holyrood Park and Duddingston Loch. It was also presumably called something else until King James VI donated an ornate ram's head snuff box to the Inn in 1580. The King used to stop here to play skittles on his way between the royal residences of Craigmillar and Holyrood. In the 19th century the ram's head was bought at auction by the Earl of Roseberry and moved to Dalmeny House. A replica was made which now sits behind the bar.

For centuries sheep grazed on the nearby pastures and were slaughtered at Duddingston. The carcasses were taken to the Fleshmarket – now a close off the Royal Mile, leaving the heads behind. These were used to make sheep heid broth or 'powsowdie', and singed sheep heid – a dish later mentioned in Mrs Beeton's *Book of Household Management*. The skulls were often used as cobblestones by the locals, while apparently singed sheep heid was occasionally still eaten in these parts until the early 1970s.

In the 18th century it was here that Maggie Dickson appeared to come back from the dead. She had supposedly been executed before her funeral entourage stopped at the Inn for a drink on their way to her burial. They must have needed many more when they saw her. In 1745 Bonnie Prince Charlie and the Jacobites almost certainly drank here before the battle of Prestonpans. Years later, the Prince was followed by Sir Walter Scott, an elder of the Duddingston kirk, which in earlier times had often clashed with the Inn on issues of morality. By 1845 the parish minister, the Rev James MacFarlane, openly tolerated the fact there were four alehouses in the village, but only on the grounds that the visiting clientele were all from Edinburgh. Later Robert Louis Stevenson also drank here as did the Rev John Thomson, another minister of the parish, better known as Jock Tamson – famous for his 'bairns'.

The Sheep Heid was a coaching inn until the arrival of the railways. It was then adopted by the Trotter's Club, a post-enlightenment club who came here to play bowls on the first Saturday of every month. In its pre-First World War heyday, members of the Trotters included 'everyone who was anyone' in Edinburgh – seemingly so long as they wore bowler hats, beards or moustaches. Women were only admitted in 2000 and numbers have now dwindled. If you come bowling today you are much more likely to bump into office nights out and birthday parties.

The Sheep Heid belonged to Major Watt of the Argyle & Sutherland Highlanders until 1951 when it became brewery-owned. It got a bad sixties makeover that has since been stripped away. The restoration work continues and has helped attract a mixed crowd of locals, students and tourists. If you visit, make sure to go to upstairs where you can eat and enjoy the panoramic view from the balcony which overlooks a courtyard, and a large beer garden that fills up in summer.

THE ATHLETIC ARMS (DIGGERS)
1–3 ANGLE PARK AVENUE EH11 2JX

There is a sketch by the comedian Billy Connolly in which Scottish football fans in Rome are reduced to ordering pints of crème de menthe – this being 'what the Pope drinks'. Earlier requests for 'a pint of Heavy' had been lost in translation. 'Heavy' is a wholly Scots expression for the dark, murky brew otherwise known as 'electric soup' or 'Eighty Shilling' – a reference to the original tax paid on a barrel. The beer was certainly heavier in alcohol than its cousin 'Seventy Shilling' or 'Special'.

For years none of this mattered in the slightest to regulars at the Diggers (officially The Athletic Arms), on Dalry Road, who would hold up their fingers as they came through the door. This pioneering use of digital communication was not to show contempt for the barman, but merely to signal how many pints were required. There was no need to specify anything else – neither the type of beer, nor the brand.

The Diggers, so-called because the gravediggers from two neighbouring cemeteries liked to drink here after a hard day's burying the dead, effectively served only one beer. Their policy was like Henry Ford's whose cars were available in every colour so long as it was black. In this case the choice was McEwans Heavy or … McEwan's Heavy. It was so much the local brew that some speculated there must be an underground pipe connecting the pub to the Fountain

Brewery 500 yards down the road. Pipe or no pipe, it always tasted beautifully fresh, thanks to having a knowledgeable bar staff and to the rapid turnover of casks in the cellar.

To be honest, there were always other beers available if you asked. There was even lager for the ladies – not something real men ever ordered. The McEwans is sadly no longer brewed, but Deuchars, which always ran a close second to the Heavy, is still available, and they now get through a fair amount of it. Sales of Deuchars turn into a flood whenever Hearts FC are playing at home at their nearby stadium – Tynecastle. The pub is packed with Jambos (as in Jam Tarts – Hearts fans) before a match, though supporters of the city's other football team – Hibs, are equally welcome.

The Diggers is a functional, no-frills pub with a black and white tiled floor, a heavily corniced ceiling and a large marble-topped bar. But for the espresso machine behind the bar and photographs of recent Hearts victories on the walls, it appears to have changed little since it was built in 1897. Among its regulars is the actor and lifelong Jambo, Ken Stott, currently playing Inspector Rebus on TV. In the TV series, Ian Rankin's fictional hero supports Hibs (although in the books it's Siobhan who's the footie fan), which meant Stott had to endure one scene wearing the other team's scarf for the first time in his life. Such are the joys of acting.

LEITH

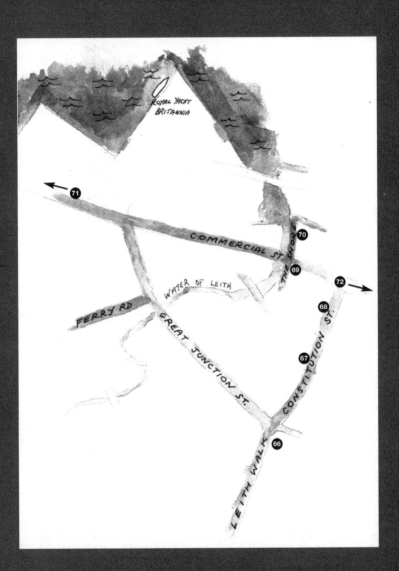

CENTRAL BAR
7 – 9 LEITH WALK EH6 8LN

'Scottish people drink spasmodically and intensely for the sake of momentary but complete release,' wrote Edwin Muir in *A Scottish Journey* in 1935. He went on to compare the 'stately shuffle' of drunks down Princes Street, with their 'music-hall swagger' along Leith Walk. If things were more raucous in Leith, it could have been due to the longer licensing hours. In good maritime tradition, pubs opened early for the dockers and sailors, and closed later. At the Boundary Bar, which sat on the edge of Edinburgh, halfway down Leith Walk, people would cross to the other side of the bar at 9.30. Now in Leith, they could drink for an extra half an hour.

There was no shortage of pubs especially at the foot of the Walk where Leith Central Station ensured a constant passing trade until it was shut in the sixties. Today, in its place, there is a supermarket car park and Job Centre. All that remains is the Central Bar, built for John Doig by the North British Railway Company in 1899 as a replacement for his earlier pub which they had knocked down to make room for the station. Doig's name is still etched on the windows and painted on a pair of whisky casks either side of the bar.

The Central Bar is a classic late-Victorian pub with a magnificent carved horseshoe bar and walls that shimmer with floor to ceiling tiles in a lustrous Ovaltine brown. There is a series of tall bevelled mirrors interspersed with tiled murals. These depict sporting scenes including an ocean-going yacht, grouse shooting and a game of golf. The tubby, bearded golfer raising his club is supposed to be the Prince of Wales – the future Edward VII.

None of this quite fits with the Central Bar's literary claim to fame. As well as featuring in the punk song 'Sixteen Years of Alcohol' by Richard Jobson, it was Begbie's local boozer – Begbie being the psychotic hardman in Irvine Welsh's nihilistic novel *Trainspotting*.

The book, set in the late eighties is written in such a dense working-class Edinburgh dialect that even well-heeled New Towners had problems getting to grips with it. 'The Fit ay Leith Walk is really likes, mobbed oot man,' declares Begbie at one point. Fortunately, the DVD came with a subtitles option.

The character of Begbie was immortalised by Robert Carlyle in the film – most of which was shot in Glasgow. Welsh himself lived round the corner in Wellington Place and must have drunk in the Central Bar as part of his research. The only time the current manager met him, however, was when she had to throw him out of the Phoenix Bar in Broughton Street where she then worked.

At the time of writing, feelings were running high about the smoking ban, with rumours that it will be enforced by special smoke wardens. One can just imagine the scene if one of them were to ask Begbie if he wouldn't mind stubbing his fag out. For all that, the Central Bar is a friendly pub where Hibs and Hearts fans have long drunk together in peace. There is also a well-established tradition of live music – mainly folk and country – at the weekends.

HOME'S BAR
182 CONSTITUTION STREET EH6 6AW

'Good beer, good cheer always on tap here.'
– says the business card of Pat Fitzgerald
owner of Home's Bar down the road from the
Port O'Leith. While Fitzgerald may not be the
greatest poet in town, he does run a fine pub.
He bought the place as a burnt-out shell in
1995 and spent the next couple of years
restoring it to the sort of bar you might find in
his home town of Mullingar.

With its pale, lemon-green walls and scuffed
lino floor it does feel like a small piece of
Ireland has landed in the heart of Leith. Not
that Home's is in any sense an 'Oirish theme
bar' – for that you need wall-to-wall Guinness
posters, a field's worth of shamrocks, loud
Celtic music and probably an Aussie barman
who's 'hoping to get to Dublin, one day'. You
also need to be part of a chain, and Home's is
not. It is a friendly independent local where
whatever 'craic' there is, is not canned, but
wholly authentic.

The building was originally a storehouse that
was converted in the early seventies into
the Spiral, the first of a long succession of
disco-pubs. By the eighties, it had become
the Bastille Lounge and Disco after 'a total
renovation'. As well as having a dance floor for
Saturday nights, the Bastille also attracted
Sunday drinkers, this being one of the few
and, possibly the only place in Leith other
than a hotel bar where you could buy a drink
on the sabbath.

The intervening years are recorded in a series
of black and white photos in the pub. In its
time, Home's has been JR's Dancing Disco
Diner, Silvana's Wine Bar, Ziggy's – Dine,
Dance and Relax, Burke & Baldie's Disco
Lounge and Bubbles – Music For You! Then
came the fire and the disco lights and boogie
nights went out for good.

Two pillars either side of the bar survived the
fire. Pat Fitzgerald would love to have them
removed given the number of times he and his
customers have smacked into them by
mistake. Then again they may have a vague
structural role – as in keeping the roof up.
Pat claims to have done little in terms of
decoration beyond painting the place. But
the shelves and cupboards are brimming with
bric-a-brac from miniature liqueurs to dusty
stoneware jars and soda syphons that he has
collected or been given. The walls are hung
with large enamelled adverts of forgotten
tobacco brands like Black Cat Virginia and
Will's Woodbines. With smoking now
banned, these will soon appear as quaint
as the hunting prints in the pubs of
rural England.

PORT O' LEITH
58 CONSTITUTION STREET EH6 6RS

The anchor above the door broadcasts the theme of this famous pub loud and clear. Step inside and you are swamped in a sea of maritime impedimenta adorning the walls. All manner of life is contained within and by midnight it resembles the *Star Wars* bar, but that shouldn't keep you away. It is all but impossible to drink alone, and even harder to leave sober.

Ships' flags completely cover the ceiling. Mannequins, caps, naval paraphernalia, postcards and banknotes from around the globe deck the walls – all gifts from passing sailors. The Port O'Leith's proprietor, Mary Moriarty, explains: 'I don't know how the tradition started, but it's now unstoppable. Every bunch of sailors leave behind a flag or cap-band, but it doesn't end there. We've also come by a lifebelt and a nameplate from the side of a ship. It's a cute little thing – 15 feet long!'

No visitor can miss the pub's figurehead – a scarlet-clad blonde taken from some large ship – now bolted to the corner facing the bar. She bears more than a passing resemblance to the redoubtable landlady herself. Yet the Port O'Leith is not just the exclusive domain of seafarers. Writers have been drawn to the place as well, including playwrights David Mamet and Steven Berkoff and the author Irvine Welsh. In his sequel entitled *Porno*, Welsh returned to his *Trainspotting* characters

ten years on. Sick Boy has acquired a pub in Leith called 'Port Sunshine' clearly based on the Port O'Leith.

When Archaos, the controversial, sell-out trapeze stars of the Edinburgh Festival visited Leith a few years ago, the cast adopted the pub as their favourite watering hole. The regular clientele were entertained by jugglers and magicians at no extra charge. Later festivals saw the arrival of the Circus of Horrors to Leith Links (directed by Peter Bidon, creator of Archaos). The members of that cast and crew soon became regulars in the best bar in the area.

The Port O'Leith welcomes artists and artisans, but the biggest compliment you can pay Mary is that her pub is indisputably – yet indefinably – Leith. She says: 'I've had ex-pats knocking on the door at 9.30 in the morning for a pie and pint, because this is the place that most reminds them of the Leith they left 25 years ago. I don't know what it is that makes a pub special, but this place has got it.'

Typical of Mary is that she wouldn't hear of any write-up without mentioning her staff, particularly her 'helper' every morning. Rachel McCaig retired after managing Noble's Bar, the neighbouring pub for 25 years. Get both ladies together and you've got the very heart of Leith and tales that would make a docker blush.

THE KING'S WARK
36 THE SHORE EH6 6QW

You might expect there to be a sandy beach in an area of Leith known as 'the Shore', but this is not the case. The Shore lies beside the bottom reaches of Edinburgh's river – the Water of Leith, as it discharges itself into the Firth of Forth. After years of neglect, the area has seen a surge of investment and now boasts a variety of restaurants and shops along with a cluster of friendly cafés and bars.

The King's Wark is a case in point. Originally it was an 18th century warehouse for royal imports and exports in and out of the bustling Port of Leith – which remained a separate township from Edinburgh until the 1920s. The building was much restored in the 1970s and given a rustic feel with the plaster stripped away to expose its massive stone walls.

Today one of the charms of the King's Wark is that you can sit over your pint of ale by candlelight at lunchtime and muse on the many comings and goings that have affected Leith over the years. In 1822, King William IV landed by ship, the first monarch to visit Scotland since Charles II in the late 1600s. The whole event was stage-managed from the start by Sir Walter Scott and had an immense impact on Scottish culture. The King, nicknamed the 'portly Hanovarian', wore a kilt, beneath which his gouty legs were encased in pink tights. The former garment caught on as members of Scottish society fell

over themselves to proclaim their 'Highland' credentials. Luckily tights did not.

The pub makes a good base from which to explore. You can stroll around the riverside or into nearby Bernard Street, which was once the commercial centre of Leith. Behind the King's Wark is Lamb's House, built in 1587 and one of the oldest surviving buildings in Leith. Nearby there are ancient vaults and cellars once full of claret shipped in from France. Further down the Shore towards the sea, you will pass the Malmaison Hotel, and discover the fully operational working docks. Outside the hotel is a harpoon gun, a reminder of the days when many whaling ships set off from Leith to the South Atlantic.

A new, modern Leith with warehouse conversion flats, office blocks and shopping malls, has been superimposed on the old. But the original Leith is still there and is perhaps best preserved in its pubs. As Isla Dewar wrote in her book *Women Talking Dirty* 'Of an evening the air was boozy. You could almost get drunk from passive drinking.'

THE SHORE BAR
3 – 4 THE SHORE EH6 6QW

**'And as for the docks,
they are magnificent to see
They comprise five docks, two piers,
1,141 yards long respectively'
William Topaz McGonagall**
The Ancient Town of Leith

As ever, Dundee's great Victorian bard and tragedian, was struck by the industrial prowess of his age – one can picture him pacing the length of the pier to measure the exact distance. Had the Shore Bar existed then, McGonagall would have given it a wide berth – he was strictly teetotal and took a dim view of the demon drink. The Shore Bar opened as a neighbourhood bar and seafood restaurant in 1984, though the building dates back to the tail end of the 18th century. It was part of a tenement that incorporates the Signal Tower of 1686, originally a windmill for making rape seed oil. In those days the street named the Shore ended right outside the bar. There was then a ramp down to a wide beach by the mouth of the Water of Leith. The beach was the setting for numerous fairs and the Leith Races which moved to Musselburgh when McGonagall's docks were built in the 19th century.

Leith had always been an important port, particularly for wine, the tax on which accounted for a third of Edinburgh's revenue before the Act of Union in 1707 when Daniel Defoe, then an English agent in the city, wrote the following: 'The Scots live by the sending of lead, wool and skins to France … and return with wine, a commodity piss'd against our walls once a year.' As each new vintage arrived, the casks would be loaded onto carts that would tour the streets tinkling their bells like an ice-cream van. People would turn up with jugs to be filled with claret for a sixpence.

In the 19th century, the Shore was lined with shops and hotels to service all the ships and ferries calling at Leith. At some point two of the shops became the Imperial Bar the cellars of which were reinforced with steel to act as an air raid shelter during the World War II. The Imperial, a popular bar with the dockers, passed through many hands until it was finally closed in the seventies. When it became the Shore Bar, the layout changed and the old snug bar was removed, but all the wood panelling lining the walls and ceiling was kept. With its rich, amber varnish, together with its brass fittings and retro lamps, the place has the feel of a classic French bistro.

On one side is a small dining room with linen tablecloths and a reclining Buddha above the door. On the other, there is an old fishing net suspended from the ceiling and a huge, floor to ceiling mirror to add space and light to the dark, cosy bar area. But for the views of the quayside and the absence of those Ricard ashtrays, one could almost be in Paris.

OLD CHAIN PIER
32 TRINITY CRESCENT EH5 3EF

In Victorian Edinburgh, passengers for Stirling would head down to the Firth of Forth for the regular steamship service up river.
The ships would dock in Trinity at the end of an old chain pier built in 1821; its thick pillars marched 500 feet out into the cold, grey waters. The pier was swept away by a storm in 1898, and all that remains are a few wooden stumps visible at low tide and a bar of the same name.

The Old Chain Pier pub sits right on the water's edge above a narrow shingle beach. As local estate agents are wont to say 'on a clear day there are fine views to the Kingdom of Fife'. In the distance you can see Kirkaldy and the hills beyond, but look closer in and you might spot seals playing by the shore. When the tide is up and there is a strong inshore breeze, the spray comes foaming up to lick the windows. During a storm, this unassuming bungalow beside the road is transformed into the most atmospheric pub in town. Years ago when the bar had its back to sea, the waves had been known to burst open a window, terrifying the staff.

Whether this ever happened to the late Betty Moss is unclear, but it would have been quite a contest to have witnessed – the power of the sea on one hand and Edinburgh's most legendary landlady on the other. When she died she left behind a wealth of stories and an old photo that hangs behind the bar. In it she appears in her customary red kimono sporting the pair of large, bamboo-framed specs she always wore. She is also unarmed and not wielding the starting pistol or the samurai sword she kept under the bar. These were whipped out at the first whiff of trouble or simply at closing time. Firing the gun or smacking the sword on the bar was Betty's eccentric take on 'time gentlemen please'.

Betty Moss ruled the Old Chain Pier from before the World War II to the early 1970s. She lived in a house across the road, and it was rumoured there was a secret passageway connecting it to the pub. No-one could work out how she would suddenly appear without warning. She was apparently married four times, always to a naval officer, swore like a trooper and had a heart of gold. She was also a magpie who collected anything she was given and then hammered it to the walls or hung it from the ceiling. The place was festooned with flags, banners, record covers, hats, posters, postcards, mirrors, gnomes, sporrans … you name it. In summer there were bathing trunks for hire at 1d a time. People either swam here or at the east pier at Granton, next door, which was lined with bathing huts. Today the thought of plunging into the Firth of Forth sends shivers down the spine, especially with the new sewage pipe nearby. The Old Chain Pier was gutted by fire in 2004. Since then, it has been completely restored with nautical maps on the ceiling and wood floors and panelling. Betty Moss left a big pair of slippers to fill, but Alison, the new landlady, is undaunted. She has already made a good start on restoring the feel of the place.

HAWES INN
NEW HALLS ROAD, SOUTH QUEENSFERRY EH30 9TA

Early in Robert Louis Stevenson's *Kidnapped*, the narrator – David Balfour – describes a walk along the Firth of Forth.

'Right in the midst of the narrows lies an islet with some ruins; on the south shore they have built a pier for the service of the ferry; and backed against a pretty garden of holly trees and hawthorns, I could see the building they call the Hawes Inn. The town of Queensferry lies further west, and the neighbourhood of the inn looked pretty lovely at that time of day, for the boat had just gone north with passengers.'

The holly trees and hawthorns have long gone and Queensferry has since expanded to subsume the Hawes Inn within its folds. The most striking change, however, is the amazing feat of engineering that passes almost directly overhead. Work on the Forth Rail Bridge was begun in 1883 by an army of Irish navvies, and completed seven years later. In true Victorian style, every detail was recorded from the 8 million rivets used, to the 8,000 workmen's caps blown into the water and later recovered.

High winds and strong drink proved a lethal cocktail for many of the 63 men who were killed building the bridge. One of the designers, Benjamin Baker, complained in 1887 that the Inn 'flourishes too well for being in the middle of our works, its attractions prove irresistible for a large proportion of our 3,000 workmen. The accident ward adjoins the pretty garden with hawthorns, and many dead and injured men have been carried there, who would have escaped had it not been for the whisky of the Hawes Inn.' Much of that whisky would have been 'Pot Still Irish' from the Cameronbridge distillery in Fife. As a 12-year-old Scotch called Cameron Brig, it still has a loyal following in the local bars and hotels.

The advent of the rail bridge did not dent the trade at the Hawes Inn and in 1893 it was extended further. The oldest part is the middle section with its crow-stepped gables and dates from the late 17th century. Ferry passengers waiting to cross continued to use the Inn for a drink or a meal. All this changed when the Queen opened the Forth Road Bridge in 1964. The Inn has a copy of that year's ferry prices displayed on its wall. There was a price for everything from cows to heifers to cars to hand-propelled perambulators. Nothing went for free, not even dead people. Corpses were charged 12/6, though what happened if you died in transit is unclear.

Today the Hawes Inn has become something of a destination restaurant with its scrubbed flagstone floors and driftwood effects on the walls. In the past it was more of a couthy, neighbourhood pub, yet it seems to be as popular as ever especially at lunch-time. When the weather's dreich and the wind is whipping in off the Forth, who could resist a pint of ale and a steaming bowl of soup. Somehow the bleak conditions outside when viewed from the warmth of the fireside makes it all taste even better.

VOLUNTEER ARMS
79 – 81 NORTH HIGH STREET, MUSSELBURGH EH21 6JE

With all the brewery-owned tied pubs and leased pubs, the genuine independent operator is as rare as the Snow Leopard according to Nigel whose family has owned and run the Volunteer Arms – also known as Stagg's – in Musselburgh from the start. It was established as a purpose-built pub in 1858 and its first landlady was Jane Montgomery. She started a chain of female licensees unbroken until Nigel took over from his aunt in 1995.

The name has changed over time and is still officially the Volunteer Arms, which it became during World War I. However, as long as anyone can recall, it has been Stagg's – named after Jimmy Stagg who married into the family in the 1920s. A saddler by trade, he was the grandson of Willie Park who won the first British Open Golf Championship in 1870.

The family were quite religious and there may have been issues of conscience over peddling the demon drink. Certainly not all the practices were good for business. One of Nigel's grandmothers would only allow men one after-work drink on a Friday before they went home and handed their pay packet to their wives. There was also a sink by the entrance where workers could wash before having a drink. One story, possibly a tall one, is of a garage mechanic whose petrol-soaked overalls caught fire when he lit his pipe. His ghost is said to haunt the pub to this day.

During the long reign of 'Aunty Cathy' from the mid-sixties onwards, the pub could well have burnt down. Punters were gathered around an old black and white TV to watch the racing when flames started sprouting

from the back of the set. With the horses nearing the final furlong, there was uproar when someone whipped the plug out. This was probably just in time given the whisky casks on the gantry and the fact that the pub's walls and ceiling are entirely panelled in dark wood.

The panelling is unchanged and a couple of casks remain behind the bar though they are now empty of Scotch. Today, like the shelves below, they form a billboard for reams of newspaper cuttings and headlines like 'NIGEL HAVERS' – a dig at the landlord and his love of indecisive blethering. Perhaps one day the real Nigel Havers will pop in for a pint if he's ever on tour at the Brunton Theatre next door. Plenty of TV actors have drunk here, particularly during the pantomime season.

Being family-owned from the beginning, Stagg's has evolved very slowly over the years. It survived the eighties and the age of the makeover completely unscathed. Yet there have been some changes, notably to the lounge bar. Briefly under Aunty Cathy, this was re-christened 'the Cocktail Lounge', though quite what exotic concoctions were on offer is unclear. Meanwhile the original jug bar has disappeared – this being where women could drink and children could buy crisps and sweeties when the local shops were shut, and the system of bells has also gone. With everyone simultaneously ringing for more drinks from every corner of the pub, it must have driven the staff demented. Nigel is hoping to reinstall the original fireplace in the main bar and lighten the dark stained panelling. Nothing radical, just an attempt to spruce up this award-winning pub in time for its 150th birthday in 2008.

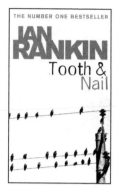

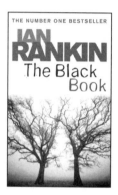

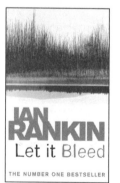

OUT NOW IN PAPERBACK AND ON AUDIO

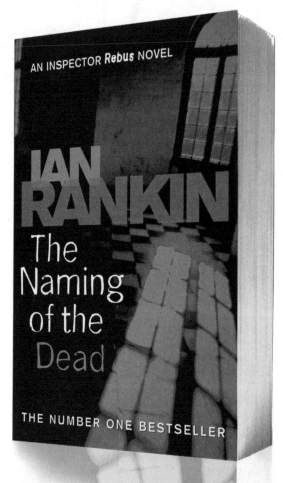

'Masterly . . . Ian Rankin's finest novel.
It is more than a crime novel, or rather, Rankin's
achievement is to show, convincingly, how crime
permeates society' **SCOTSMAN**

Brewed by hand in Edinburgh

The Caledonian has been brewing beer in Edinburgh since 1869 and is the last survivor of the city's 40 breweries. Our direct fired, open coppers are the last in use in the UK and all our beers are brewed using whole hop flowers, rather than concentrates.

Simple ingredients and traditional brewing skills makes for great beer — brewed the Caledonian way. No wonder the Inspector is such a fan!

Deuchars IPA
Winner of 40 awards since 1991 — loved by Rebus, Rankin and beer fans everywhere

Caledonian 80
Recognised as the definitive '80 shilling' ale Malty, smooth, creamy and quite delicious

Golden Promise
The UK's first certified organic beer and 5 times winner at the Soil Association Organic Food awards

Caledonian XPA
Pale gold, full flavoured with a bittersweet finish. Decidedly moreish!